angeli caffè
pizzapastapanini

ALSO BY EVAN KLEIMAN

Cucina del Mare

Cucina Fresca
(WITH VIANA LA PLACE)

Pasta Fresca
(WITH VIANA LA PLACE)

Cucina Rustica
(WITH VIANA LA PLACE)

evan kleiman

angeli caffè
pizzapastapanini

heavenly recipes from the city of angels' most beloved caffè

photographs by Michael Hodgson
illustrations by Ann Field

WILLIAM MORROW AND COMPANY, INC.   NEW YORK

Library of Congress Cataloging-in-Publication Data

Kleiman, Evan.
        Angeli Caffè's pizza, pasta, panini: heavenly recipes from the City of Angels' most beloved caffè/Evan Kleiman.
        p.   cm.
      Includes index.
ISBN 0-688-14269-9
1. Pizza. 2. Cookery (Pasta). 3. Sandwiches. 4. Cookery, Italian. 5. Angeli Caffè (Restaurant). 6. Los Angeles (Calif.)—Cookery. I. Title.
TX770.P58K54 1997
641.5945—dc20   96–30279
                                                CIP

Printed in the United States of America

First Edition

1 2 3 4 5 6 7 8 9 10

BOOK DESIGN BY Ph.D

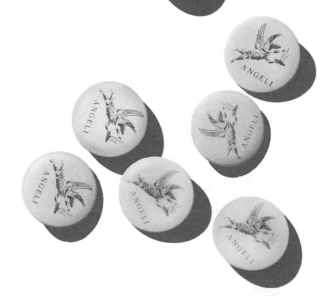

This book is dedicated to

John and Carla Strobel
for their partnership in creation

Tony Gramaglia
whose extraordinary spirit continues to envelop us with love

Edith Kleiman
the Mom to us all, but especially me

acknowledgments

I want to thank those who gave Angeli life and continue to keep it moving forward. You have all given so much of yourselves to keep us flying all these years. I love all of you for it.

To all the Angels who gave in that most concrete of ways so that Angeli could fly (a special thanks to N.D., the first to fork over the green so many years ago).

To my current staff
Ted, Kathy, Miguel, Ivana, Orlando, Mario, Reinaldo, Javier A., Javier P., Victor, Bruno, Rolando, Adolfo, Areli, Jose, Andrea, Laura, Crystal, Nick, Tony, Kim, David, Nadia, Benedetta, Raul, Erica, Amador

To those driving Angels
Mitch, John, Jack, Jim, Leonard, Bob, Peter

And those from the past who have gone on to touch others with your gifts but whose presence still lingers
Ilana, Brent, Frank, Brigit, Brown, Mary Ann, Tom, Cosme, Elvia, Kathy St., Gigi, Sandy, Cindy, Rochelle, Kathy V., Susan, Gary, Lia, Lars, Jennifer, Peter, Harry, Dean, Mark, Michelle, Julio,

and, of course, "the group," Liz, Ivan, Albert, Steve, John, Nancy, Sadie, Cleo, Julie

To those who eat the dream every week
Ruth and Mickey, the Franklins, Tony and Gail, Steve and Sims, Jonathan, Marcelle, the Winters, Michael and Andy, the Greggs, Jan and David, Mark, Sal

Special thanks to my editors on this project, Kathleen Hackett and Ann Bramson, whose patience with this crazy restaurant lady was endless. Thanks also to Maureen and Eric Lasher, my agents, who have the unenviable job of keeping me focused on the task at hand. Big hugs to Kathy Ternay, chef of Angeli Caffè and Brigit Legérè Binns, for their amiable support under pressure during recipe testing and general organization of the manuscript. A special joy of this project was reuniting with Michael Hodgson and Clive Piercy of the design firm P*h*.D. It was great to burrow through twelve years of design work and watch them turn it all into something new and vibrant.

Also loving appreciation to the women of The Immaculate Heart Center in Montecito for giving me silence and sanctuary. Special hugs to Oldways for allowing me the opportunity to reexperience the food of southern Italy, so crucial for this book.

contents

introduction

It seems odd to be writing an Angeli book after writing so many cookbooks on other subjects. Odd because angels are now so ubiquitous and my connection with them grew from such an innocent decision . . . to name the restaurant after the city in which I was born and grew up, Los Angeles, City of Angels.

Over the years it has become truly that for me—a city of angels. Since the inception of Angeli Caffè on Melrose in 1984, those of us in the immediate Angeli family have considered ourselves a band of angels with our T-shirt wings on our backs. The true angels, however, are those who gave us their confidence through initial investment capital and those who walk through our doors and have allowed us to share our food and our lives with them all these years.

People always ask how Angeli started. Those who have dreams of making it big in the restaurant business want a blueprint that will lead them to success. My answer is always the same—just get yourself on the road and follow your heart.

The heart of Angeli Caffè, of course, is the food. The foods presented in this book are those you've been eating since childhood. The ones you return to again and again when you need to comfort yourself. They're simple foods that are a joy to make and a pure pleasure to eat. The Italian triad of pizza, pasta, and panini has an inherent informality and a familiarity so intimate to us that we almost never think of them as "ethnic" or "exotic." Pizza, pasta, and panini are the comfort carbohydrates, the foods we make when all we want is to cook to please ourselves. This collection of recipes provides you with a glimpse of how we at Angeli help our clientele achieve that gratification. But first take a stroll down the road that led to Angeli.

My initiation into Italian culture, language, and food was a seduction of simplicity, a simplicity that for some reason I instinctively understood and embraced. Perhaps it was because the Los Angeles of the sixties and early seventies was rather simple. There were lots of open spaces to hang out in and dream. There was trust among neighbors; we didn't lock our doors. There was the heat, the sun, and the ocean, which together created an underlying sense of sensuality and the ease of quenching desires. Sounds a lot like Italy to me. The fact that I was barely seventeen on my first trip to Italy, an only child of a single parent and hungry for roots, also played a part. I was captivated by the intense connection of the Italian people to their land and its food. My fascination continued to grow until it eventually became my life. Maybe that is why my favorite description of my food is that of Faith Willinger (author of *Eating in Italy* and *Red, White & Greens*) who called it "cucina rustica from the provincia of California"—rustic Italian cooking from the region of California. For as interested as I am in the authenticity of Italian cuisine, I live and cook in California, a happenstance that never ceases to be a blessing. The wealth and quality of the ingredients available is staggering, while the prices allow us to be generous.

I grew up cooking, and, despite many years following scholarly pursuits, I always loved to work with my hands. So it was natural for me to help pay my way through college by cooking. At first, I worked for local caterers, but over time, as my knowledge and confidence grew, I developed my own clientele. The two rivers of my life, cooking and an intellectual fascination with Italian literature and film, flowed side by side for many years. Eventually I had to make a choice. Working ten hours a day in a producer's office, then returning home to cook until four in the morning for my catering business couldn't go on indefinitely. The kitchen won.

As luck would have it, I came of age professionally in a time and place when everything was possible. The idea of women in professional kitchens had gained more acceptance than ever before. Interest in *la cucina Italiana* was growing too. The seventies saw the opening of many "northern Italian" restaurants that purported to

serve a "lighter" cuisine than the Italo-American fare commonly encountered in restaurants at that time. For me, these restaurants were problematic, being neither light nor, from an authentically regional point of view, terribly northern. However, they did prime an audience

for an Italian dining experience that could be elegant and a cuisine that could be regarded seriously.

The early stages of my professional career flew by and I quickly had opportunities and success that in another time and place might have taken years. Within two years of beginning to work as a restaurant chef, I had already presided over the opening of a new establishment, Verdi Ristorante di Musica, as head chef and was ready to open my own place. I suppose my natural workaholic tendencies soon convinced me that I might as well work a hundred hours a week, or more, in search of my own dream rather than in the service of someone else's!

It's 1995 and as I stand watching photographer/author Naomi Duguid zoom in on the single metal street sign tacked onto the whitewashed wall of a humble old palazzo, I think to myself, how appropriate. I started my journey on the Angeli road more than fourteen years ago. I've followed its twists and turns, sometimes tortuous ones, sometimes smooth, easy curves. But there on a small, perfectly human-scaled street in Gallipoli, I came face to face with my journey—both the one already taken and the one yet to begin—how right.

on the road of angels

I left my restaurant job as head chef of Verdi to spend a contemplative period collaborating with Viana La Place on our first book, *Cucina Fresca*. This period of quiet was invaluable. Writing down my thoughts about the food I had been cooking and researching for the previous few years helped crystallize its importance in my life. It also convinced me that I had something to offer that would be unique in my hometown. Before too long I was itching to get back into a professional kitchen; this time it would be my own culinary point of view of Italy on the menu. I started developing menus of my favorite foods from time spent in Italy, and with my head in books reading about the foods of Italy. Small dinner parties showcasing the menu items followed. I kept talking the dream, and then a series of coincidences came together to make it reality.

I met John Strobel, another young restaurant professional ready to fly. We hit it off and decided to start the year-long process that resulted in the opening of Angeli Caffè-Pizzeria. Our discussions were quite informal and always over food. We shared our thoughts on the business and about what we thought we could do that others before us hadn't. We found a young attorney to put together a prospectus that would allow us to begin to raise capital to create our dream. We began the grueling process of raising money by asking everyone we knew to invest. After many twists and turns, we had enough in the bank to start looking for a space. Melrose Avenue at the time was just beginning to be an interesting street. Young entrepreneurs seemed to be drawn there to create their own quirky visions. We joined them to develop one of the only areas in LA at that time that became a zone for walking. The street became known for its artsy neon, eccentric stores, and even more flamboyant pedestrians.

A major impetus to opening a restaurant is a desire to combine the talents and tastes of one's group of friends. In this I think we were supremely lucky. Los Angeles is a magnet for creative young people from all over the world who want to make their mark. Ann Field, illustrator, and Clive Piercy and Michael Hodgson, graphic designers, had recently come from London; project architect Michele Saee had just arrived from Florence, where he had spent the last fifteen years. All were part of a group from Europe living and working in LA and imparting a new sense of design. So there we were, a fertile group ready to give birth to something new.

Who would design the space? The only architects who would understand our incredibly low budget were friends, Thom Mayne and Michael Rotondi of Morphosis, one of the leading progressive firms of the 1980s.

Just as the food is simple, so are the two very small connecting rooms that make up Angeli Caffè on Melrose. The space is more like Los Angeles than Italy. I have always been opposed to the idea of creating a theme park–like environment in reference to a culinary culture. Instead, I have always tried to be referential to the way you *feel* while you are eating at a simple Italian caffè or trattoria. The rooms are often spare, with just the basic amenities. The fact that many caffès in Italy are ensconced in centuries-old buildings means a replica cannot be re-created in late twentieth-century Los Angeles, so why try?

Originally we acquired one storefront with a thousand square feet. The idea was to present *pizza a taglio*, pan pizza displayed in the window the way you see it

all over Italy. But the more conversations we had, and the more comfortable we became with the new business, the more our ideas developed. So we went from the concept of a simple counter with twenty-four seats and *pizza al taglio* in the window to thirty-eight seats in a tiny dining room designed like an abstract chapel. When I first approached Michael and Thom about designing a little caffè, the preeminent image in my mind was of a chapel filled with niches and candles. (I would later wander the streets of East LA, stopping at Guatemalan and El Salvadoran *panaderías* to find bakers who would make giant bread angels to hang in those niches.) All is modern and spare, with the exterior facade as the one grand gesture. A sculptural steel facade, now rusted to a beautiful velvety patina, is bolted to the front of the building.

the opening

In December of 1984, Angeli Caffè-Pizzeria opened. Trattoria Angeli followed in 1987 and Angeli Mare in 1989. Angeli Caffè-Pizzeria was the first casual Italian caffè serving regional rustic food in a hip, modern environment. And it was as if Los Angeles had been waiting for us. I remember looking out through the kitchen door one night and seeing a mob of people spilling off the sidewalk in front of the Caffè into the street. I thought there had been an accident. No, John calmly told me, they were

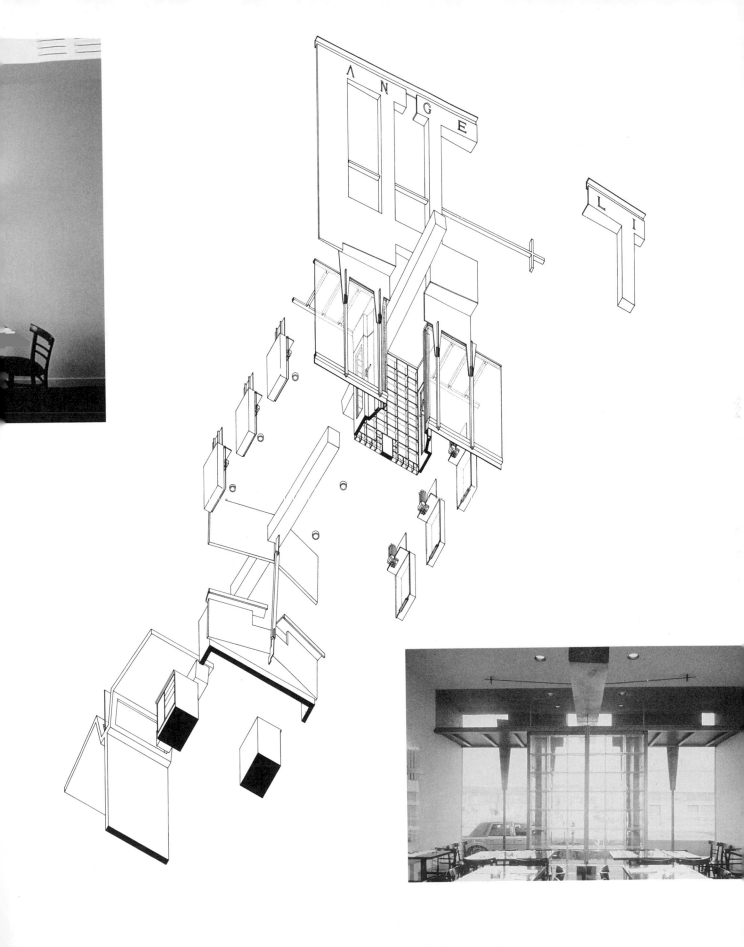

ANGELI

CAFFÉ/PIZZERIA · CATERING · HOME DELIVERY (213) 936 9867
MON-SAT 11.30 AM-11.30 PM, SUN 4 - 10.30 PM · RESERVATIONS ACCEPTED
ANGELI, 7274/6 MELROSE AVE., L.A., CA 90046 · (213) 936 9086

waiting to eat our food. In the beginning, the only experienced restaurant professional besides John and me was Pasquale Morra, our pizza chef. Even Pasquale's wife, Anna, who was to become my first assistant, had never cooked before, not even at home. The youngest of a large Neapolitan family, she left school at fifteen to work and missed the opportunity to have kitchen time with her mother. So there we were, young and ready to kill ourselves with work. The family began to grow.

the family of angels

The intimacy we create between customer and server, customer and cook, and, especially, among the family of management, servers, and cooks, is not something that can be planned. A huge percentage of our customers are regulars, eating with us more than once a week. Many of them have done so every week since we first opened our doors. I'm often told that being at the Caffè is as close as they can get to eating in their own kitchens—but the food is better and there are no dishes to wash. I believe it is the simplicity of our approach that allows people to share our food so often. The food is primally satisfying without being demanding on the palate or the intellect; it is a relief in the frenetic world of urban stress that is Los Angeles today.

pizza, pasta, panini

The earthly simplicity that is emblematic of Angeli and has been imitated by many (making us feel amazingly flattered) starts with the food. All the good that comes to us flows from that center. It is the reason we are here spending a good chunk of our lives serving those who walk through our doors. The spare rustic quality of the food is what first strikes our customers. Sometimes I watch their faces when the food is put in front of them, simple and unadorned. Occasionally I see a perplexed look. I know they are thinking, Is that all? But I wait until they start eating. Their expressions quickly change to surprise and a relaxed satisfaction. The realization that the dish before them is full of flavor and often bright with primary colors creates Angeli addicts. Angeli food is "roots food" served in a city where roots are hard to see or find, and where we all are called upon constantly to create our own. It is a *cucina* reduced to the most basic of elements, food that developed out of poverty from a group of insular regional cultures that were the Italian city-states of old. In cooking classes I often describe it as reductive. Food reduced to basic taste components where nothing is covered up; complexity simply for its own sake is banished.

No matter who we are or where we come from, we nearly always bring a complex set of subtle, primal expectations to our time at the table. There is no disappointment as sharp as frustration during a meal. Conversely, there are few pleasures as complete as when that first bite melds into our sense memories to allow us to gratify our basic desires. We let go, if only momentarily, of our troubles and daily concerns. At Angeli we are proud of the part we play in giving this simple pleasure to others.

pizza and other savories from the angeli ovens

When Angeli first opened in 1984, our *pizzaiòlo* was Pasquale Morra, a young man recently arrived from Naples who had already spent a few years paying his dues in a variety of pizzerie in his hometown. When Pasquale eventually left Angeli, he left us the legacy of the "dough mystique"—the idea that craft comes from repeating "the making" over and over . . . and over. Often we make up to three hundred pounds of dough a day at Angeli Caffè, the equivalent of more than twelve hundred pizze or loaves of *pane*, bread. One learns over time that the end result of this constant repetition of the same moves, the same ingredients, the same amounts is pure craft—something that becomes more than the sum of the parts. I remember Pasquale telling me once that the "secret" is all in knowing when to turn off the mixer; I thought he was being secretive. But now I understand that the pizza maker can recognize minute changes in the dough. It is like living with a fleshy woman for years and years. You begin to respect and appreciate all the dimples and wrinkles. And you learn that these characteristics all have a story to tell you about your product.

Recently I read an article by John Thorne in his newsletter *Simple Cooking*, in which he came to the conclusion that authenticity is more than the banal repetition of ingredients and techniques. It is the act of creating something with familiarity and integrity to a point where it reaches it own nexus of authenticity. This is what we do at Angeli. Ours is not a slavish attempt to re-create the famous street food of Naples. It is our own Neapolitan-style pizza developed over many years and with much sharing between eater and maker.

The crust is slightly crunchy upon first bite, but the inner crumb is yielding and delicate. Its lightness means that less topping often gives a better result, as too baroque an amount tends to weigh the dough down.

Naturally, a selection of filled pizze are on our regular and party menus everyday. Calzone, folded-over pizze, are the most familiar of this variety. Double-decker pizze, such as Sfincione or Pizza Rustica, also appear frequently, as do a variety of savory tarts and, of course, focaccia.

Both our pizza and focaccia doughs are fairly soft. The softer the dough, the more delicate and soft the finished product. Doughs that are tough and elastic often make crunchy, brittle crusts.

Making the doughs is very simple, but if you have the opportunity to attend a couple of classes where you can see the process and feel the dough, you will feel much less intimidated.

Two indispensable tools for making pizza are available in many gourmet shops and hardware stores. The first is a pizza stone, or unglazed quarry tiles, which should be put onto the bottom shelf or floor of a cold oven and preheated along with the oven. Baking pizza on a stone cooks the dough quickly and most closely reproduces the slightly charred taste of a pizza baked in a wood-fired oven. The idea is to cook the pizza as quickly as possible; the intense heat the stone is able to absorb, then radiate, speeds this process. In a traditional wood-fired oven, a pizza cooks in only one minute or so. In a typical home oven at a temperature of 500 degrees, it usually takes between six to ten minutes.

The second tool that you must have for making pizza at home is a wooden pizza peel, a sort of giant wooden spatula, on which the pizza is formed and topped. It is the most trouble-free way of sliding the pizza onto the stone. The secret to sliding the pizza easily off the peel is to work flour well into the peel before laying the dough on top. Always check the topped pizza to see that it slides around freely on the peel before you try to slip it onto the hot baking stone. If part of the pizza dough is stuck, throw a bit more flour underneath the pizza until it releases itself.

The biggest "secret" to successful pizza, however, is to make the dough frequently, so you always have some on hand. Keep some in the freezer or refrigerator so that the last-minute decision to make some bread or pizza doesn't involve a big production. And the more you do it, the easier and more natural it becomes—like most things in life.

pizza

Pizza is such a playful, accessible food that we never seem to tire of it. The start of each shift at Angeli begins with a staff pizza. For over a decade, twice a day, the pie makes its appearance, and the pizza invariably disappears in seconds. One minute the pan is full; the next, the slices disappear. The toppings are as infinite as the pleasures. Here are a few of our ideas that you may enjoy.

Pasta di Pane per la Pizza (Pizza Dough)

Makes 1¾ pounds dough, enough for four 8-inch pizze

A SIMPLE, SOFT PIZZA DOUGH that results in a delicate crust, crisp on the outside and yielding within. The dough will keep in the refrigerator for approximately two days or in the freezer for up to one month (thaw overnight in the refrigerator before using).

1 PACKAGE (1 SCANT TABLESPOON) ACTIVE DRY YEAST

¼ CUP LUKEWARM WATER

3¼ CUPS UNBLEACHED ALL-PURPOSE FLOUR, PLUS MORE IF NECESSARY

1½ TEASPOONS SALT

3 TABLESPOONS EXTRA-VIRGIN OLIVE OIL

1 CUP COLD WATER

To make the pizza dough using a food processor

In a small bowl, sprinkle the yeast over the warm water. Let it fizz for about 5 minutes. Put the flour, yeast mixture, salt, olive oil, and cold water into the bowl of a food processor fitted with the metal blade, and process until the dough forms a ball. The dough should be fairly soft. If not, add a bit more water. If it is too sticky, add a bit more flour and process for another minute.

Sprinkle a work surface with a little flour, and transfer the dough to the floured surface. Knead for 2 to 3 minutes, or until smooth and elastic. Shape the dough into a ball.

Rub the inside of a large mixing bowl with a little olive oil. Transfer the dough to the bowl, turn once to coat with the oil, and cover with plastic wrap or a kitchen towel. Let the dough rest in a warm place for about 15 minutes.

To make the pizza dough by hand

In a small bowl, sprinkle the yeast over the warm water. Let it fizz for about 5 minutes. In a large bowl, combine the yeast mixture, 2½ cups of the flour, the salt, olive oil, and cold water. Mix with a wooden spoon until you have a thick batter.

Sprinkle a work surface generously with flour. Transfer the batter to the floured surface. Knead the remaining 1 cup flour, a little at a time, into the dough, kneading for 8 to 10 minutes in all. The dough should be soft and elastic but not sticky; add a little bit more flour if needed. Shape the dough into a ball.

Rub the inside of a large mixing bowl with a little olive oil. Transfer the dough to the bowl, turn once to coat, and cover with plastic wrap or a clean kitchen towel. Let the dough rest in a warm place for about 15 minutes.

To shape the dough
Sprinkle a work surface with flour. Divide the dough into quarters, and roll each piece into a tight, smooth ball, kneading it to push the air out of it. Place the dough balls on a lightly floured surface, cover them with a clean kitchen towel, and let rise for an hour. Or place them on a floured towel on a cookie sheet, cover with a towel, and let rise in the refrigerator overnight. Let refrigerated dough sit out at room temperature for 5 to 10 minutes before shaping the dough into a pizza.

To shape the pizze
Place 1 ball of dough on a lightly floured work surface or a floured peel. Sprinkle a little more flour on top of the ball. Using your fingertips, press the dough ball down evenly into a large flat disk about ½ inch thick. Lift the dough and lay it over the back of the fist of one hand. Place your other fist underneath the dough so your fists are almost touching. Now gently stretch the dough by moving your fists away from each other; each time you perform this stretching move, rotate the dough. Continue stretching and rotating until the round of dough is about ¼ inch thick and measures about 9 inches across. The dough is now ready for whichever topping you choose. Repeat with the remaining dough balls.

Pizza Aglio e Olio

GARLIC AND OIL

Makes one 8-inch pizza

THE SIMPLEST PIZZA IS NEARLY A CRACKER BREAD. The fewer moist ingredients placed atop the circle of dough, the crisper finish the pizza will have. Sometimes we use this pizza as if it were a plate, topping it with simply sauced spaghetti or a summery salad. It makes a delicious accompaniment to savory dips like hummus or olive pastes.

DOUGH FOR ONE 8-INCH PIZZA (SEE PAGE 18), STRETCHED OUT TO A 9-INCH ROUND

2 TABLESPOONS EXTRA-VIRGIN OLIVE OIL

5 TO 6 GARLIC CLOVES, PEELED AND THINLY SLICED

Place a pizza stone or unglazed tiles on the lowest oven rack. Preheat the oven to 500°F.

Sprinkle some flour onto a wooden pizza peel. Gently lift the stretched dough round onto it. Drizzle the olive oil over the pizza and rub it lightly into the surface with your fingers. With a pizza cutter or a sharp knife, make $^1/_2$-inch slashes about $^1/_2$ inch apart, all around the edges and throughout the center of the pizza, to stop the pizza from puffing up in the oven (since it has no heavy topping to weight it down). Scatter the sliced garlic evenly over the pizza.

Shake the wooden peel gently back and forth to make sure the pizza is not stuck to it, and quickly slide the pizza onto the hot baking stone. Bake for 5 minutes, then check the pizza for air bubbles. If any have formed, prick them with a pizza cutter or a knife. Bake until the pizza edges are golden, about 4 more minutes. Using a metal peel or spatula, remove the pizza from the oven.

Pizza Umbria

ONION, SAGE, PECORINO ROMANO, PARMESAN

Makes one 8-inch pizza

UMBRIAN CUISINE HAS A STARK, EARTHY CHARACTER, the result of rustic juxtapositions of the most elemental ingredients. This minimalist offering mixes the bite of charred raw onion and the earthy taste of sage with two cheeses to provide a satisfying accompaniment to braised greens or a seasonal salad.

> DOUGH FOR ONE 8-INCH PIZZA (SEE PAGE 18), STRETCHED OUT TO A 9-INCH ROUND
>
> 2 THIN SLICES ONION, SEPARATED INTO RINGS
>
> 1 TABLESPOON COARSELY CHOPPED FRESH SAGE
>
> 2 TABLESPOONS GRATED PECORINO ROMANO CHEESE
>
> 2 TABLESPOONS GRATED ITALIAN PARMESAN CHEESE

Place a pizza stone or unglazed tiles on the lowest oven rack. Preheat the oven to 500°F.

Sprinkle some flour onto a wooden pizza peel. Gently lift the stretched dough round onto it. Scatter the onion over the pizza. Sprinkle the fresh sage over, then sprinkle the two cheeses evenly on top.

Shake the wooden peel gently back and forth to make sure the pizza is not stuck to it, then quickly slide the pizza onto the hot baking stone. Bake until the edges are golden, about 8 minutes. Using a metal peel or spatula, remove the pizza from the oven.

Pizza Napoletana

TOMATO SAUCE, GARLIC, ANCHOVY, OREGANO

Makes one 8-inch pizza

THE CLASSIC TOPPING OF THE PIZZERIE OF NAPLES is enjoyable precisely because it is not masked by rich, melted cheese. The simple tastes of tomato, garlic, and oregano are set off by a drizzle of assertive olive oil. Our body-conscious customers lap this up, as they do all our cheeseless pizzas.

DOUGH FOR ONE 8-INCH PIZZA (SEE PAGE 18), STRETCHED OUT TO A 9-INCH ROUND

1/4 CUP UNCOOKED TOMATO SAUCE FOR PIZZA (SEE PAGE 220)

2 TO 4 GARLIC CLOVES, PEELED AND THINLY SLICED

1 ANCHOVY PACKED IN SALT, RINSED, BONES REMOVED, AND TORN INTO PIECES (OPTIONAL)

2 PINCHES DRIED OREGANO

EXTRA-VIRGIN OLIVE OIL FOR DRIZZLING

1 TABLESPOON CHOPPED FRESH ITALIAN PARSLEY (OPTIONAL)

Place a pizza stone or unglazed tiles on the lowest oven rack. Preheat the oven to 500°F.

Sprinkle some flour onto a wooden pizza peel. Gently lift the stretched dough round onto it. Use the back of a spoon to spread the tomato sauce over the pizza, leaving a 1/2-inch border of dough all around. Scatter the garlic and the anchovy, if desired, evenly over the pizza. Sprinkle with the oregano and drizzle a liberal amount of oil over the pizza.

Shake the wooden peel gently back and forth to make sure the pizza is not stuck to it, and quickly slide the pizza onto the hot baking stone. Bake until the edges are golden, about 8 minutes. Using a metal peel or spatula, remove the pizza from the oven.

Scatter the parsley over the pizza if desired.

Pizza Puttanesca

TOMATO SAUCE, GARLIC, OLIVES, CAPERS, ANCHOVY

Makes one 8-inch pizza

THE PIQUANT INGREDIENTS OF THE FAMOUS ROMAN PASTA sauce create a strongly flavored pizza that is perfect as an accompaniment to cocktails or a beer on a hot summer day. Because there is no cheese to obscure the ingredients this pizza is particularly rich with color as the black and green of olives and capers contrast with the deep red of the tomato sauce. A fortunate morning snack when recovering from a bit too much to drink the night before.

DOUGH FOR ONE 8-INCH PIZZA (SEE PAGE 18), STRETCHED OUT TO A 9-INCH ROUND

1/4 CUP UNCOOKED TOMATO SAUCE FOR PIZZA (SEE PAGE 220)

2 TO 4 GARLIC CLOVES, PEELED AND THINLY SLICED

8 KALAMATA OR MOROCCAN OIL-CURED OLIVES, PITTED AND TORN IN HALF

1 TEASPOON CAPERS

1 ANCHOVY PACKED IN SALT, RINSED, BONES REMOVED, AND TORN INTO PIECES

RED CHILE PEPPER FLAKES TO TASTE

PINCH OF DRIED OREGANO

EXTRA-VIRGIN OLIVE OIL FOR DRIZZLING

Place a pizza stone or unglazed tiles on the lowest oven rack. Preheat the oven to 500°F.

Sprinkle some flour onto a wooden pizza peel. Gently lift the stretched dough round onto it. Use the back of a large spoon to spread the tomato sauce over the pizza, leaving a ½-inch border of dough all around. Scatter the garlic, olives, capers, anchovy, hot pepper flakes, and oregano over the pizza. Drizzle on a bit of olive oil.

Shake the wooden peel back and forth gently to make sure the pizza is not stuck to it, then quickly slide the pizza onto the hot baking stone. Bake until the edges are golden, about 8 minutes. Using a metal peel or spatula, remove the pizza from the oven.

Pizza Provenzale

EGGPLANT, ONION, TOMATO, ANCHOVY, OLIVES

Makes one 8-inch pizza

A PIZZA TO MAKE DURING SUMMER MONTHS when eggplants are at their sweet, creamy best and tomatoes are bursting with flavor. A luscious combination that recalls hot summer days along the sea.

OLIVE OIL FOR FRYING

1 JAPANESE EGGPLANT, ENDS TRIMMED AND CUT LENGTHWISE INTO $1/4$-INCH-THICK SLICES

1 SMALL ONION, PEELED AND COARSELY CHOPPED

DOUGH FOR ONE 8-INCH PIZZA (SEE PAGE 18), STRETCHED OUT TO A 9-INCH ROUND

1 RIPE ROUND TOMATO OR 2 RIPE ROMA TOMATOES, STEM END(S) REMOVED AND CUT INTO $1/4$-INCH-THICK SLICES

1 TO 2 ANCHOVIES PACKED IN SALT, RINSED, BONES REMOVED, AND TORN INTO PIECES

8 KALAMATA OR MOROCCAN OIL-CURED OLIVES, PITTED AND TORN IN HALF

Place a pizza stone or unglazed tiles on the lowest oven rack. Preheat the oven to 500°F.

Pour enough olive oil into a deep frying pan to come ½ inch up the side and heat until very hot but not smoking. Add the eggplant slices a few at a time, without crowding the pan, and fry until golden brown on both sides. Drain on paper towels.

Discard all but 1 tablespoon of the oil from the pan. Sauté the onion in the oil until it is translucent and soft. Remove from the heat.

Sprinkle some flour onto a wooden pizza peel. Gently lift the stretched dough round onto it. Spread the sautéed onion over the pizza. Lay the tomato slices over the onion in a circular pattern, covering the dough but leaving a ½-inch border all around. Distribute the anchovy pieces evenly over the pizza, then arrange the eggplant slices on top. Scatter the olives over the eggplant.

Shake the wooden peel gently back and forth to make sure the pizza is not stuck to it, then quickly slide the pizza onto the hot baking stone. Bake until the edges are golden, about 8 minutes. Using a metal peel or spatula, remove the pizza from the oven.

Pizza al Pesto

PESTO, GARLIC, PINE NUTS, ONION, PARMESAN

Makes one 8-inch pizza

A FAVORITE WITH BOTH SOPHISTICATED eaters and strangely enough, those ten and under. A painless way to get little ones to eat some green food. The garlicky pesto sauce is topped with thin slices of onion and pine nuts. A generous dusting of grated Parmesan cheese finishes off the pizza when it comes steaming from the oven.

DOUGH FOR ONE 8-INCH PIZZA (SEE PAGE 18), STRETCHED OUT TO A 9-INCH ROUND

1/4 CUP BASIL PESTO (SEE PAGE 225)

2 TO 4 GARLIC CLOVES, PEELED AND THINLY SLICED

2 TEASPOONS PINE NUTS

2 THIN SLICES ONION, SEPARATED INTO RINGS

GRATED ITALIAN PARMESAN CHEESE FOR SPRINKLING

Place a pizza stone or unglazed tiles on the lowest oven rack. Preheat the oven to 500°F.

Sprinkle some flour onto a wooden pizza peel. Gently lift the stretched dough round onto it. Use the back of a spoon to spread the pesto liberally over the pizza, leaving a 1/2-inch border of dough all around. Scatter the garlic and pine nuts over the pesto. Scatter on the onion, and finish by sprinkling Parmesan cheese over all.

Shake the wooden peel gently back and forth to make sure the pizza is not stuck to it, and quickly slide the pizza onto the hot baking stone. Bake until the edges are golden, about 8 minutes. Using a metal peel or spatula, remove the pizza from the oven. Finish the pizza with an additional dusting of Parmesan cheese.

Pizza Margherita

TOMATO SAUCE, BASIL, MOZZARELLA
Makes one 8-inch pizza

THE QUEEN OF ALL PIZZAS. If there had to be only one, this would be it. Simply a round of delicate dough, topped with sweet tomato sauce, mozzarella, and fresh basil—but what alchemy! This is the ultimate comfort food when it seems that nothing will satisfy a jaded palate. At Angeli we use an American-style low-moisture mozzarella. At first we experimented with fresh mozzarella, but we found that when it melts, it becomes too watery for our customers' tastes. Try different brands of mozzarella until you find one that you like. The ideal is a cheese that will melt softly and smoothly without stringiness or oil separation.

DOUGH FOR ONE 8-INCH PIZZA (SEE PAGE 18), STRETCHED OUT TO A 9-INCH ROUND

¼ CUP UNCOOKED TOMATO SAUCE FOR PIZZA (SEE PAGE 220)

5 LEAVES FRESH BASIL

GRATED ITALIAN PARMESAN CHEESE FOR SPRINKLING

3½ OUNCES MOZZARELLA CHEESE, SLICED ¼ INCH THICK

Place a pizza stone or unglazed tiles on the lowest oven rack. Preheat the oven to 500°F.

Sprinkle some flour onto a wooden pizza peel. Gently lift the stretched dough round onto it. Use the back of a spoon to spread the tomato sauce over the pizza, leaving a ½-inch border of dough all around. Scatter the basil over the sauce. Sprinkle with the Parmesan cheese and lay the slices of mozzarella evenly over the top, leaving a bit of space between them.

Shake the wooden peel gently back and forth to make sure the pizza is not stuck to it, and quickly slide the pizza onto the hot baking stone. Bake until the edges are golden and the cheese is bubbling, about 8 minutes. Using a metal peel or spatula, remove the pizza from the oven.

Pizza Angeli

TOMATO SAUCE, GARLIC, BASIL, SMOKED MOZZARELLA

Makes one 8-inch pizza

SMOKED MOZZARELLA, OR *SCAMORZA AFFUMICATA* AS it is called in Italy, leaves its mark in any dish imbued with its distinctive smoky flavor. One of my favorite memories of walking the streets of New York was a stroll taken with one of my editors, Ann Bramson. As we turned onto Sullivan Street, passing Joe's Dairy, we were enveloped in smoke pouring up into the street from a basement workshop. I immediately recognized the smell and dragged her down the stairs to buy a freshly smoked cheese for eating later in the day. Smoked mozzarella and thin slices of fresh garlic turn Pizza Margherita into a pie with a more sophisticated taste.

DOUGH FOR ONE 8-INCH PIZZA (SEE PAGE 18), STRETCHED OUT TO A 9-INCH ROUND

¼ CUP UNCOOKED TOMATO SAUCE FOR PIZZA (SEE PAGE 220)

1 TO 2 MEDIUM GARLIC CLOVES, PEELED AND THINLY SLICED

6 TO 7 LEAVES FRESH BASIL

4 THIN SLICES SMOKED MOZZARELLA CHEESE (ABOUT 3 OUNCES), TORN INTO BITE-SIZED PIECES

Place a pizza stone or unglazed tiles on the lowest oven rack. Preheat the oven to 500°F.

Sprinkle some flour onto a wooden pizza peel. Gently lift the stretched dough round onto it. Use the back of a spoon to spread the tomato sauce over the pizza, leaving a ½-inch border of dough all around. Scatter the sliced garlic and basil over the pizza, then lay the pieces of smoked mozzarella evenly over the top.

Shake the wooden peel gently back and forth to make sure the pizza is not stuck to it, and quickly slide the pizza onto the hot baking stone. Bake until the edges are golden, about 8 minutes. Using a metal peel or spatula, remove the pizza from the oven.

Pizza alla Checca

BASIL, MOZZARELLA, GARLIC, FRESH TOMATOES

Makes one 8-inch pizza

USING FRESH TOMATOES INSTEAD OF TOMATO SAUCE makes this pizza—named after the modern Roman classic, spaghetti checca—lighter on the palate and the tummy than the traditional Pizza Margherita.

DOUGH FOR ONE 8-INCH PIZZA (SEE PAGE 18), STRETCHED OUT TO A 9-INCH ROUND

5 LEAVES FRESH BASIL, COARSELY CHOPPED

3½ OUNCES MOZZARELLA CHEESE, CUT INTO ¼-INCH-THICK SLICES

2 TO 3 CLOVES GARLIC, PEELED AND THINLY SLICED

2 RIPE ROMA TOMATOES OR 1 RIPE ROUND TOMATO, STEM END(S) REMOVED AND CUT INTO ¼-INCH-THICK SLICES

EXTRA-VIRGIN OLIVE OIL FOR DRIZZLING

Place a pizza stone or unglazed tiles on the lowest oven rack. Preheat the oven to 500°F.

Sprinkle some flour onto a wooden pizza peel. Gently lift the stretched dough round onto it. Sprinkle the basil over the dough, then distribute the mozzarella evenly over the top, leaving a ½-inch border all around. Arrange the garlic and tomatoes in a circular pattern on the pizza, and finish by drizzling with a generous amount of olive oil.

Shake the wooden peel gently back and forth to make sure the pizza is not stuck to it, and quickly slide the pizza onto the hot baking stone. Bake until the edges are golden, about 8 minutes. Using a metal peel or spatula, remove the pizza from the oven.

Pizza alla Parmigiana

ARTICHOKES, EGGPLANT, TOMATO SAUCE, SMOKED MOZZARELLA

Makes one 8-inch pizza

THERE IS SOMETHING ABOUT THE COMBINATION of smoked mozzarella, artichoke hearts, and sautéed eggplant that becomes positively luscious when baked atop pizza dough. A longtime favorite of employees and customers alike.

4 BABY ARTICHOKES OR 4 FROZEN ARTICHOKE HEARTS, THAWED AND QUARTERED, OR $\frac{1}{4}$ CUP MARINATED ARTICHOKE HEARTS, DRAINED

3 TABLESPOONS EXTRA-VIRGIN OLIVE OIL

1 JAPANESE EGGPLANT, ENDS TRIMMED AND CUT INTO $\frac{1}{2}$-INCH DICE

DOUGH FOR ONE 8-INCH PIZZA (SEE PAGE 18), STRETCHED OUT TO A 9-INCH ROUND

$\frac{1}{4}$ CUP UNCOOKED TOMATO SAUCE FOR PIZZA (SEE PAGE 220)

4 THIN SLICES SMOKED MOZZARELLA CHEESE (ABOUT 3 OUNCES), TORN INTO BITE-SIZED PIECES

GRATED ITALIAN PARMESAN CHEESE FOR SPRINKLING

Place a pizza stone or unglazed tiles on the lowest oven rack. Preheat the oven to 500°F.

If using fresh artichokes, remove the stems and all coarse outer leaves. Trim any remaining tough dark green parts from the bases. Blanch the artichokes in boiling salted water until tender, about 7 minutes. Drain, let cool, and cut into quarters.

In a medium skillet, heat the olive oil over medium-high heat. Sauté the eggplant, turning to brown evenly, until tender and golden. Drain on paper towels.

Sprinkle some flour onto a wooden pizza peel. Gently lift the stretched dough round onto it. Use the back of a spoon to spread the tomato sauce over the pizza, leaving a $\frac{1}{2}$-inch border of dough all around. Lay the smoked mozzarella evenly over the pizza. Distribute the eggplant and the artichokes evenly over the top, then sprinkle with a generous amount of Parmesan cheese.

Shake the wooden peel gently back and forth to make sure the pizza is not stuck to it, and quickly slide the pizza onto the hot baking stone. Bake until the edges are golden, about 8 minutes. Using a metal peel or spatula, remove the pizza from the oven.

Pizza Primaverile

ARTICHOKES, SPINACH, LEEK, TOMATO SAUCE, ASPARAGUS

Makes one 8-inch pizza

AROUND THE SPRINGTIME HOLIDAYS OF PASSOVER AND EASTER, I like to add an egg to the center of this pizza. It provides a beautiful reminder of the rebirth of the season and gives additional richness to this vegetarian dish. Simply break a raw egg carefully over the vegetables in the center of the pizza and then slide it into the oven with a prayer. The egg "fries" atop the pizza in the intense heat of the oven and creates a special treat. Traditionally pizzas topped with egg in Italy are called *capricciosa*, meaning capricious.

4 BABY ARTICHOKES OR 4 FROZEN ARTICHOKE HEARTS, THAWED AND QUARTERED

1/4 POUND TENDER SPINACH, STEMS TRIMMED AND WELL WASHED

KOSHER SALT TO TASTE

1 LARGE LEEK (WHITE PART ONLY), WELL RINSED AND THINLY SLICED

2 TABLESPOONS EXTRA-VIRGIN OLIVE OIL

DOUGH FOR ONE 8-INCH PIZZA (SEE PAGE 18), STRETCHED OUT TO A 9-INCH ROUND

1/4 CUP UNCOOKED TOMATO SAUCE FOR PIZZA (SEE PAGE 220) (OPTIONAL)

10 MEDIUM OR THIN ASPARAGUS TIPS

GRATED PARMESAN CHEESE FOR SPRINKLING

Place a pizza stone or unglazed tiles on the lowest oven rack. Preheat the oven to 500°F.

If using raw artichokes, remove the stems and all coarse outer leaves. Trim any remaining tough dark green parts from the bases. Blanch the artichokes in boiling salted water until tender, about 7 minutes. Drain, let cool, and cut into quarters.

Put the spinach in a saucepan with just the water that clings to the leaves and add salt to taste. Cover and cook over low heat until tender, then drain well in a colander. When the spinach is cool enough to handle, squeeze dry. Coarsely chop and set aside.

In a small skillet, sauté the leek in the olive oil over medium-low heat until softened and almost translucent. Set aside.

Sprinkle some flour onto a wooden pizza peel. Gently lift the stretched dough round onto it. Use the back of a spoon to spread the tomato sauce, if desired, over the pizza, leaving a

½-inch border of dough all around. Distribute the spinach and artichokes evenly over the pizza. Top with the leek, and finish by scattering the asparagus tips over the pizza.

Shake the wooden peel gently back and forth to make sure the pizza is not stuck to it, and quickly slide the pizza onto the hot baking stone. Bake until the edges are golden, about 8 minutes. Using a metal peel or spatula, remove the pizza from the oven. Sprinkle with Parmesan cheese.

Pizza ai Peperoni Rossi

MOZZARELLA, SWEET RED PEPPERS, GARLIC, CAPERS, OLIVES, OREGANO

Makes one 8-inch pizza

THE COMBINATION OF SWEET RED PEPPERS and salty capers and olives is a treat to be savored. This is an exceptionally pretty pizza with the color contrasts of red peppers, white cheese, and black olives, all set off by the deep-green parsley. What intrigues me about this pie is that it manages to be very light while bursting with flavor.

DOUGH FOR ONE 8-INCH PIZZA (SEE PAGE 18), STRETCHED OUT TO A 9-INCH ROUND

2½ TO 3 OUNCES MOZZARELLA CHEESE, CUT INTO ¼-INCH-THICK SLICES

½ LARGE RED BELL PEPPER, STEM, SEEDS, AND TOUGH WHITE MEMBRANES REMOVED AND CUT INTO THIN STRIPS

1 GARLIC CLOVE, PEELED AND THINLY SLICED

1 TEASPOON CAPERS

1 RIPE ROMA TOMATO OR ½ RIPE ROUND TOMATO, STEM END REMOVED AND CUT INTO ½-INCH DICE

5 KALAMATA OR MOROCCAN OIL-CURED OLIVES, PITTED AND HALVED

PINCH OF DRIED OREGANO

EXTRA-VIRGIN OLIVE OIL FOR DRIZZLING

1 TABLESPOON COARSELY CHOPPED FRESH ITALIAN PARSLEY (OPTIONAL)

Place a pizza stone or unglazed tiles on the lowest oven rack. Preheat the oven to 500°F.

Sprinkle some flour onto a wooden pizza peel. Gently lift the stretched dough round onto it. Distribute the mozzarella evenly over the pizza, leaving a ½-inch border all around. Lay the red pepper over the cheese, then scatter the garlic and capers over the top. Arrange the tomato on the pizza, scatter the olives over, and sprinkle with the oregano. Finish by drizzling with a generous amount of olive oil.

Shake the wooden peel gently back and forth to make sure the pizza is not stuck to it, and quickly slide the pizza onto the hot baking stone. Bake until the edges are golden, about 8 minutes. Using a metal peel or spatula, remove the pizza from the oven. Sprinkle the parsley over the pizza if desired.

Pizza al Caprino

GOAT CHEESE, CARAMELIZED GARLIC, SUN-DRIED TOMATOES, CAPERS, OREGANO

Makes one 8-inch pizza

FOR YEARS I WAS SO COMMITTED TO serving only absolutely authentic Italian food at the restaurants that I refused to even consider the possibility that we could put goat cheese on a pizza. Eventually I caved in to pressure from customers and my waitstaff. My friend and colleague Nancy Silverton-Peel, of LA's La Brea Bakery/Campanile, says this is her favorite pizza; I guess it was worth compromising on this one. We simply put the ingredients of our most popular cheese antipasto atop the dough and bake it.

DOUGH FOR ONE 8-INCH PIZZA (SEE PAGE 18), STRETCHED OUT TO A 9-INCH ROUND

3 OUNCES FRESH GOAT CHEESE, CRUMBLED

10 TO 15 CLOVES CARAMELIZED GARLIC (SEE PAGE 228)

5 SUN-DRIED TOMATOES PACKED IN OIL, CUT INTO STRIPS

1 TEASPOON CAPERS

PINCH OF DRIED OREGANO

EXTRA-VIRGIN OLIVE OIL FOR DRIZZLING

Place a pizza stone or unglazed tiles on the lowest oven rack. Preheat the oven to 500°F.

Sprinkle some flour onto a wooden pizza peel. Gently lift the stretched dough round onto it. Scatter the crumbled goat cheese evenly over the pizza, leaving a ½-inch border all around. Distribute the garlic, sun-dried tomatoes, and capers evenly over the goat cheese. Sprinkle with the oregano and drizzle with a generous amount of olive oil.

Shake the wooden peel gently back and forth to make sure the pizza is not stuck to it, and quickly slide the pizza onto the hot baking stone. Bake until the edges are golden, about 8 minutes. Using a metal peel or spatula, remove the pizza from the oven.

Pizza Paradiso

FONTINA, GORGONZOLA, SUN-DRIED TOMATOES

Makes one 8-inch pizza

A TREAT FOR ANYONE WHO ENJOYS strong, complex flavors. The nutty smoothness of the Fontina acts as a balance to the stronger Gorgonzola. When I make this pizza for myself, I often substitute walnuts for the sun-dried tomatoes.

DOUGH FOR ONE 8-INCH PIZZA (SEE PAGE 18), STRETCHED OUT TO A 9-INCH ROUND

3 OUNCES ITALIAN FONTINA CHEESE, SLICED ¼ INCH THICK

1½ OUNCES GORGONZOLA CHEESE

5 SUN-DRIED TOMATOES PACKED IN OIL, CUT INTO THIN STRIPS (PLUS A LITTLE OF THE TOMATO OIL)

Place a pizza stone or unglazed tiles on the lowest oven rack. Preheat the oven to 500°F.

Sprinkle some flour onto a wooden pizza peel. Gently lift the stretched dough round onto it. Arrange the Fontina cheese evenly over the pizza, leaving a ½-inch border all around. Crumble the Gorgonzola evenly over the Fontina. Distribute the sun-dried tomatoes evenly over the pizza and finish by drizzling with a little of the oil from the sun-dried tomatoes.

Shake the wooden peel gently back and forth to make sure the pizza is not stuck to it, and quickly slide the pizza onto the hot baking stone. Bake until the edges are golden, about 8 minutes. Using a metal peel or spatula, remove the pizza from the oven.

Pizza Tutto Crudo

GARLIC, SALAD OF MOZZARELLA, ARUGULA, AND TOMATO

Makes one 8-inch pizza

THE ULTIMATE SUMMER SALAD of fresh mozzarella, tomato, and arugula is tossed in our favorite olive oil of the moment and served atop a Pizza Aglio e Olio. The juices of the sweet tomatoes mingle with olive oil and soak into the crispy pizza. Yum! The edible plate is savored upon finishing the salad.

3 OUNCES FRESH MOZZARELLA CHEESE, DRAINED AND CUT INTO $\frac{1}{4}$-INCH DICE

1 TO 2 TABLESPOONS EXTRA-VIRGIN OLIVE OIL, PLUS EXTRA FOR DRIZZLING

KOSHER SALT AND FRESHLY GROUND BLACK PEPPER TO TASTE

DOUGH FOR ONE 8-INCH PIZZA (SEE PAGE 18), STRETCHED OUT TO A 9-INCH ROUND

5 TO 6 GARLIC CLOVES, PEELED AND THINLY SLICED

SMALL HANDFUL OF TENDER ARUGULA, TOUGH STEMS REMOVED AND COARSELY CHOPPED

3 RIPE ROMA TOMATOES, QUARTERED LENGTHWISE AND SLICED $\frac{1}{4}$ INCH THICK

Place a pizza stone or unglazed tiles on the lowest oven rack. Preheat the oven to 500°F.

In a medium bowl, toss the mozzarella with the olive oil and salt and pepper to taste. Set aside.

Sprinkle some flour onto a wooden pizza peel. Gently lift the stretched dough round onto it. Drizzle a bit of olive oil over the pizza and rub it lightly into the surface with your fingers. With a pizza cutter or a sharp knife, make $\frac{1}{2}$-inch slashes, about $\frac{1}{2}$ inch apart, all around the edges and throughout the center of the pizza, to stop the pizza from puffing up in the oven (since it has no heavy topping to weight it down). Scatter the sliced garlic evenly over the pizza.

Shake the wooden peel gently back and forth to make sure the pizza is not stuck to it, and quickly slide the pizza onto the hot baking stone. Bake for 5 minutes, then check the pizza for air bubbles. If any have formed, prick them with a pizza cutter or a knife. Bake until the pizza edges are golden, about 4 more minutes. Using a metal peel or spatula, remove the pizza from the oven.

Add the arugula and tomatoes to the bowl with the mozzarella and quickly toss to mix. Serve the salad mixture on the pizza.

Pizza Vegetariana

SPINACH, ZUCCHINI, EGGPLANT, TOMATO SAUCE, MUSHROOMS, FRESH TOMATO, MOZZARELLA
Makes one 8-inch pizza

A POPULAR OFFERING AT ANGELI CAFFÈ. A more "American-style" pie topped with a wide variety of vegetables. When we add salami and prosciutto to this baroque pizza, we call it L'Americana.

1/4 POUND TENDER SPINACH, STEMS TRIMMED AND WELL WASHED

KOSHER SALT TO TASTE

1/4 CUP EXTRA-VIRGIN OLIVE OIL

1 MEDIUM ZUCCHINI, ENDS TRIMMED AND SLICED 1/4 INCH THICK

1 JAPANESE EGGPLANT, ENDS TRIMMED, HALVED LENGTHWISE, AND SLICED 1/4 INCH THICK

DOUGH FOR ONE 8-INCH PIZZA (SEE PAGE 18), STRETCHED OUT TO A 9-INCH ROUND

1/4 CUP UNCOOKED TOMATO SAUCE FOR PIZZA (PAGE 220)

5 MEDIUM MUSHROOMS, TRIMMED, WIPED CLEAN, AND SLICED

1 RIPE ROUND TOMATO OR 2 RIPE ROMA TOMATOES, STEM END(S) REMOVED, HALVED LENGTHWISE, AND CUT INTO 1/4-INCH-THICK SLICES

2 OUNCES MOZZARELLA CHEESE, CUT INTO 1/4-INCH-THICK SLICES

Place a pizza stone or unglazed tiles on the lowest oven rack. Preheat the oven to 500°F.

Put the spinach in a saucepan with just the water that clings to the leaves and add salt to taste. Cover and cook over low heat until tender. Drain well in a colander. When the spinach is cool enough to handle, squeeze dry. Coarsely chop and set aside.

In a medium skillet, heat the olive oil over medium-high heat. Sauté the zucchini and eggplant slices, in batches, turning to brown evenly, until tender and golden. Drain on paper towels.

Sprinkle some flour onto a wooden pizza peel. Gently lift the stretched dough round onto it. Use the back of a spoon to spread the tomato sauce over the pizza, leaving a 1/2-inch border of dough all around. Scatter the mushrooms and the sautéed zucchini and eggplant evenly over the pizza. Arrange the tomatoes over the pizza and scatter on the chopped spinach over the tomatoes. Lay the slices of mozzarella evenly over the top.

Shake the wooden peel gently back and forth to make sure the pizza is not stuck to it, and quickly slide the pizza onto the hot baking stone. Bake until the edges are golden, about 8 minutes. Using a metal peel or spatula, remove the pizza from the oven.

Pizza Autunnale

ACORN SQUASH, SHIITAKE, PORTOBELLO, AND CREMINI MUSHROOMS, RADICCHIO, SUN-DRIED TOMATO PESTO, ROSEMARY

Makes one 8-inch pizza

A SUPER-HEALTHY PIZZA RICH with the subtle colors and flavors of fall. You can use any combination of mushrooms you like here; about 1 cup of sliced mushrooms will do.

1/2 SMALL ACORN SQUASH OR 1/4 POUND BANANA SQUASH

2 TABLESPOONS EXTRA-VIRGIN OLIVE OIL

3 MEDIUM SHIITAKE MUSHROOMS, STEMS CUT OFF, WIPED CLEAN, AND SLICED

2 PORTOBELLO MUSHROOMS, STEMS REMOVED, WIPED CLEAN, AND SLICED

3 MEDIUM CREMINI MUSHROOMS, TRIMMED, WIPED CLEAN, AND SLICED

1 TEASPOON FINELY CHOPPED FRESH THYME

1/2 SMALL HEAD RADICCHIO, CORE REMOVED

DOUGH FOR ONE 8-INCH PIZZA (SEE PAGE 18), STRETCHED OUT TO A 9-INCH ROUND

2 TABLESPOONS SUN-DRIED TOMATO PESTO (SEE PAGE 224) (OPTIONAL)

1 SPRIG ROSEMARY, LEAVES ONLY, FINELY CHOPPED

GRATED ITALIAN PARMESAN CHEESE FOR SPRINKLING

Preheat the oven to 375°F.

Place the squash cut side down on a lightly oiled baking sheet. Bake until just tender when pierced with a sharp knife, approximately 30 minutes. Let cool slightly. When the squash is cool enough to handle, peel off the skin and cut the flesh into 1/4-inch-thick slices. Set aside.

Place a pizza stone or unglazed tiles on the lowest oven rack, and increase the oven temperature to 500°F.

In a medium skillet, heat the olive oil. Add all the mushrooms and the thyme and sauté over medium-high heat until they are tender and have given up most of their liquid. Set aside.

Blanch the radicchio in boiling salted water for 1 minute. Drain and coarsely chop.

Sprinkle some flour onto a wooden pizza peel. Gently lift the stretched dough round onto it. If desired, use the back of a spoon to spread the sun-dried tomato pesto in a thin layer over the pizza, leaving a 1/2-inch border of dough all around. Scatter the mushrooms evenly over the pizza, then arrange the sliced squash over them. Finish by scattering the radicchio over the squash and sprinkle the rosemary over all.

Shake the wooden peel gently back and forth to make sure the pizza is not stuck to it, then quickly slide the pizza onto the hot baking stone. Bake until the edges are golden, about 8 minutes. Using a metal peel or spatula, remove the pizza from the oven. Sprinkle with grated Parmesan cheese.

Pizza ai Tre Formaggi

RICOTTA, MOZZARELLA, PARMESAN, BASIL, PROSCIUTTO

Makes one 8-inch pizza

A SYMPHONY OF CHEESES THAT IS EQUALLY DELICIOUS with the addition of Fontina or, for the truly decadent, a bit of mascarpone. The salty sweetness of prosciutto relieves the richness of the assorted cheeses. For a vegetarian alternative, we substitute cooked spinach for the prosciutto.

DOUGH FOR ONE 8-INCH PIZZA (SEE PAGE 18), STRETCHED OUT TO A 9-INCH ROUND

1/2 CUP RICOTTA CHEESE

5 LEAVES FRESH BASIL, COARSELY CHOPPED

1 THIN SLICE PROSCIUTTO, TORN INTO SMALL BITE-SIZED PIECES

2 OUNCES MOZZARELLA CHEESE, CUT INTO 1/4-INCH-THICK SLICES

GRATED ITALIAN PARMESAN CHEESE FOR SPRINKLING

Place a pizza stone or unglazed tiles on the lowest oven rack. Preheat the oven to 500°F.

Sprinkle some flour onto a wooden pizza peel. Gently lift the stretched dough round onto it. Using a spoon, drop the ricotta over the base of the pizza in small dollops, leaving a 1/2-inch border all around. Scatter over the basil and prosciutto, and then distribute the mozzarella evenly over the pizza. Finish by sprinkling the Parmesan cheese over the top.

Shake the wooden peel gently back and forth to make sure the pizza is not stuck to it, and quickly slide the pizza onto the hot baking stone. Bake until the edges are golden, about 8 minutes. Using a metal peel or spatula, remove the pizza from the oven.

Pizza Salsicce

SAUSAGE, CARAMELIZED ONIONS, FONTINA, MOZZARELLA

Makes one 8-inch pizza

THIS PIZZA STARTED OFF AS ONE OF OUR WINTER SPECIALS, but now no one will let me take it off the menu. I think it's the combination of the crumbled fennel-studded sausage meat and the sweet caramelized onions that explains our customers' attachment to this savory pie.

1 TEASPOON EXTRA-VIRGIN OLIVE OIL

1 SWEET ITALIAN SAUSAGE, CASING REMOVED

DOUGH FOR ONE 8-INCH PIZZA (SEE PAGE 18), STRETCHED OUT TO A 9-INCH ROUND

1/4 CUP CARAMELIZED ONIONS (SEE PAGE 229)

3 THIN SLICES ITALIAN FONTINA CHEESE (ABOUT 1 1/2 OUNCES), TORN INTO BITE-SIZED PIECES

1 1/2 OUNCES MOZZARELLA CHEESE, SLICED 1/4 INCH THICK

GRATED ITALIAN PARMESAN CHEESE FOR SPRINKLING

Place a pizza stone or unglazed tiles on the lowest oven rack. Preheat the oven to 500°F.

In a medium skillet, heat the olive oil over medium heat. Sauté the sausage, crumbling the meat with a fork or a spatula, until no pink remains. Drain on paper towels.

Sprinkle some flour onto a wooden pizza peel. Gently lift the stretched dough round onto it. Arrange the caramelized onions over the pizza, then scatter the sausage over. Distribute the Fontina and mozzarella cheeses evenly over the pizza, then sprinkle with the Parmesan cheese.

Shake the wooden peel gently back and forth to make sure the pizza is not stuck to it, and quickly slide the pizza onto the hot baking stone. Bake until the edges are golden, about 8 minutes. Using a metal peel or spatula, remove the pizza from the oven.

Pizza Invernale

RED ONION, POTATO, PANCETTA, FONTINA

Makes one 8-inch pizza

A FAVORITE WINTERTIME OFFERING is this comforting combination of potatoes, onion, and pancetta, topped with the nutty creaminess of Fontina cheese.

2 TABLESPOONS PLUS 2 TEASPOONS EXTRA-VIRGIN OLIVE OIL

1 SMALL RED ONION, PEELED, THINLY SLICED, AND SEPARATED INTO RINGS

$1/2$ MEDIUM RUSSET POTATO, SCRUBBED

1 SLICE PANCETTA OR BACON, COARSELY CHOPPED

DOUGH FOR ONE 8-INCH PIZZA (SEE PAGE 18), STRETCHED OUT TO A 9-INCH ROUND

3 SLICES ITALIAN FONTINA CHEESE (ABOUT 2 OUNCES), TORN INTO BITE-SIZED PIECES

GRATED ITALIAN PARMESAN CHEESE FOR SPRINKLING

Place a pizza stone or unglazed tiles on the lowest oven rack. Preheat the oven to 500°F.

In a medium skillet, combine 2 tablespoons of olive oil, 2 tablespoons water, and the sliced onion and cook over medium heat, stirring occasionally, until all the liquid has evaporated. Reduce the heat to low and cook until the onion has caramelized slightly. Set aside.

Meanwhile, cook the potato in simmering salted water until just tender. Drain and let cool slightly, then peel and cut into $1/4$-inch-thick slices. Set aside.

In a medium skillet, heat the remaining 2 teaspoons olive oil over medium heat. Sauté the pancetta or bacon until crisp and golden. Drain on paper towels.

Sprinkle some flour onto a wooden pizza peel. Gently lift the stretched dough round onto it. Arrange the potato slices over the pizza, leaving a $1/2$-inch border all around. Distribute the pancetta or bacon and the onion evenly over the potato. Top with the Fontina cheese and finish by sprinkling with the Parmesan cheese.

Shake the wooden peel gently back and forth to make sure the pizza is not stuck to it, then quickly slide the pizza onto the hot baking stone. Bake until the edges are golden, about 8 minutes. Using a metal peel or spatula, remove the pizza from the oven.

Pizza ai Funghi

TOMATO SAUCE, MUSHROOMS, PROSCIUTTO, MOZZARELLA

Makes one 8-inch pizza

THE FIRST TIME I HAD A PIZZA TOPPED WITH MUSHROOMS was in Perugia, during my days at L'Università per Stranieri. A hole-in-the-wall trattoria tucked into Etruscan walls several feet thick served pizza that redefined the word for me. I was confronted with a pie heaped so high with mushrooms I could barely see the dough. This experience taught me that eating pizza with a fork and knife prolonged the pleasure and gave the simple street food the respect it deserves.

DOUGH FOR ONE 8-INCH PIZZA (SEE PAGE 18), STRETCHED OUT TO A 9-INCH ROUND

¼ CUP UNCOOKED TOMATO SAUCE FOR PIZZA (SEE PAGE 220)

5 MEDIUM MUSHROOMS, TRIMMED, WIPED CLEAN, AND THINLY SLICED

1 THIN SLICE PROSCIUTTO, TORN INTO SMALL BITE-SIZED PIECES

3 THIN SLICES MOZZARELLA CHEESE (ABOUT 1½ OUNCES), TORN INTO BITE-SIZED PIECES

Place a pizza stone or unglazed tiles on the lowest oven rack. Preheat the oven to 500°F.

Sprinkle some flour onto a wooden pizza peel. Gently lift the stretched dough round onto it. Use the back of a spoon to spread the tomato sauce over the pizza, leaving a ½-inch border of dough all around. Scatter the mushrooms and prosciutto evenly over the pizza. Distribute the mozzarella evenly over the top.

Shake the wooden peel gently back and forth to make sure the pizza is not stuck to it, and quickly slide the pizza onto the hot baking stone. Bake until the edges are golden, about 8 minutes. Using a metal peel or spatula, remove the pizza from the oven.

Pizza Quattro Stagioni

TOMATO SAUCE, PARMESAN, HERBS, SALAMI, PROSCIUTTO, MUSHROOM, ARTICHOKE HEART, MOZZARELLA
Makes one 8-inch pizza

ONE OF MY FAVORITES. THE FOUR SEASONS PIZZA is divided into quadrants by thin strips of dough, then each section is filled with ingredients that represent a different season. Children really enjoy the idea of creating separate spaces on a pizza and letting their imagination fly to fill them. Adults (big children?) like the variety within one pie.

DOUGH FOR ONE 8-INCH PIZZA (SEE PAGE 18), STRETCHED OUT TO A 9-INCH ROUND

$^1/_4$ CUP UNCOOKED TOMATO SAUCE FOR PIZZA (SEE PAGE 220)

5 LEAVES FRESH BASIL, COARSELY CHOPPED

$1^1/_2$ TEASPOONS GRATED ITALIAN PARMESAN CHEESE

3 MEDIUM GARLIC CLOVES, PEELED AND THINLY SLICED

$^1/_2$ TEASPOON DRIED OREGANO

EXTRA-VIRGIN OLIVE OIL FOR DRIZZLING

1 SLICE SALAMI, TORN INTO BITE-SIZED PIECES

1 SLICE PROSCIUTTO, TORN INTO BITE-SIZED PIECES

1 MEDIUM MUSHROOM, TRIMMED, WIPED CLEAN, AND SLICED $^1/_4$ INCH THICK

1 ARTICHOKE HEART, CANNED OR THAWED FROZEN, QUARTERED

2 OUNCES MOZZARELLA CHEESE, SLICED $^1/_4$ INCH THICK

Place a pizza stone or unglazed tiles on the lowest oven rack. Preheat the oven to 500°F.

With a pizza cutter or a sharp knife, shave off a $^1/_4$-inch strip from one side of the dough round. Stretch and roll it between your hands into a narrow rope that is double the diameter of the pizza. Set aside.

Sprinkle some flour onto a wooden pizza peel. Gently lift the stretched dough round onto it. Use the back of a spoon to spread the tomato sauce over the pizza, leaving a $^1/_2$-inch border of dough all around.

Tear the dough rope in half and use it to divide the pizza into 4 equal sections. Scatter the basil over the first section and sprinkle with the Parmesan. Scatter the sliced garlic over the second section, sprinkle with the oregano, and drizzle with a little olive oil. Distribute the salami and prosciutto evenly in the third section. Scatter the mushroom and artichoke heart over the fourth section. Lay the slices of mozzarella evenly over all the sections except the one containing the garlic and oregano.

Shake the wooden peel gently back and forth to make sure the pizza is not stuck to it, and quickly slide the pizza onto the hot baking stone. Bake until the edges are golden, about 8 minutes. Using a metal peel or spatula, remove the pizza from the oven.

Pizza Siciliana

TOMATO SAUCE, MOZZARELLA, PROSCIUTTO, ROASTED RED PEPPERS, OLIVES, OREGANO

Makes two 8-inch pan pizzas

THIS RECIPE AND THE ONE THAT FOLLOWS are two of my favorite pan pizzas. The dough is the same one we use for our individual pizzas; the difference in thickness is achieved by doubling the amount of dough used for the thin-crust pizzas. If you prefer the look of a more irregular shape, you can make these thicker pizzas without using a cake pan. Just pat and stretch the ball of dough into an eight-inch round, lay it on a floured peel, and bake it on a stone. Our *pizzaiòlo* at Angeli Mare, Marcello Mele, delighted the staff every time he made these thicker pizzas for staff lunch. Customers in the know would wait around until the very end of lunch, hoping to be offered a piece. Some things we like to save for ourselves!

> 1 recipe Pizza Dough (see page 18), divided into 2 balls and allowed to rise
>
> ½ cup Uncooked Tomato Sauce for Pizza (see page 220)
>
> 6 ounces mozzarella cheese, sliced
>
> 4 thin slices prosciutto, torn into small bite-sized pieces
>
> 2 Roasted Red Peppers (see page 227), torn into bite-sized pieces
>
> 20 Kalamata or Moroccan oil-cured olives, pitted and halved
>
> 2 teaspoons dried oregano
>
> Extra-virgin olive oil for drizzling

Place a pizza stone or unglazed tiles on the lowest oven rack. Preheat the oven to 500°F.

Place 1 ball of dough on a lightly floured work surface. Sprinkle a little more flour on top of the ball. Using your fingertips, press the ball down into a large flat disk about ¾ inch thick. Lift the dough and lay it over the back of the fist of one hand. Place your other fist underneath the dough so your fists are almost touching. Now gently stretch the dough by moving your fists away from each other; each time you perform this stretching move, rotate the dough. Continue stretching and rotating until the round of dough is about ½ inch thick and measures about 8 inches across. Press the dough into a lightly oiled 8-inch cake pan. Repeat with the remaining dough ball. Then dimple the dough in each pan with your fingertips, pressing firmly and allowing a thicker rim of dough to build up around the edge.

Use the back of a spoon to spread half the tomato sauce over the bottom of each pizza. Distribute the mozzarella over the pizzas, then scatter the prosciutto and roasted peppers evenly over them. Scatter the olives over the top, sprinkle on the oregano, and finish by drizzling with a generous amount of olive oil.

Bake until the crust is golden, 10 to 12 minutes. Remove the pizzas from the oven.

Pizza ai Frutti di Mare

TOMATO SAUCE, SHRIMP, CLAMS, MUSSELS, SQUID, HERBS

Makes one 8-inch pizza

WHEN WE FIRST SERVED THIS PIZZA, we presented it crowded with the seafood in the shell, but it proved to be too exotic a presentation for many eaters. If you're cooking for a carefree crowd and want to really have fun, simply throw a couple of clams and mussels—shell and all—on the pizza and let them pop open in the oven. Their delicate juices will immediately be absorbed by the pizza dough.

DOUGH FOR ONE 8-INCH PIZZA (SEE PAGE 18), STRETCHED OUT TO A 9-INCH ROUND

1/4 CUP UNCOOKED TOMATO SAUCE FOR PIZZA (SEE PAGE 220)

EXTRA-VIRGIN OLIVE OIL FOR DRIZZLING

HANDFUL OF CHOPPED FRESH ITALIAN PARSLEY

2 TABLESPOONS FRESH OREGANO LEAVES, COARSELY CHOPPED

10 FRESH BASIL LEAVES, COARSELY CHOPPED

10 COOKED MEDIUM SHRIMP, PEELED, DEVEINED, AND CUT IN HALF LENGTHWISE

10 MANILA CLAMS, STEAMED OPEN AND MEAT REMOVED (SEE NOTE)

10 MUSSELS, STEAMED OPEN AND MEAT REMOVED (SEE NOTE)

1/4 POUND CLEANED SQUID, CUT INTO 1/4-INCH-THICK RINGS

Place a pizza stone or unglazed tiles on the lowest oven rack. Preheat the oven to 500°F.

Sprinkle some flour onto a wooden pizza peel. Gently lift the stretched dough round onto it. Use the back of a spoon to spread the tomato sauce over the pizza, leaving a 1/2-inch border of dough all around. Drizzle a little olive oil over the dough, then scatter the herbs evenly over it. Arrange the seafood over the herbs.

Shake the wooden peel gently back and forth to make sure the pizza is not stuck to it, and quickly slide the pizza onto the hot baking stone. Bake until the pizza edges are golden and all the seafood is cooked, 6 to 8 minutes. Using a metal peel or spatula, remove the pizza from the oven.

Note: To open the clams or mussels, place in a dry skillet large enough to hold them in one or two layers. Cover the pan and cook over high heat just until the shells pop open, 2 to 3 minutes. Set aside to cool slightly, then remove the meat from the shells.

Pizza alla Romagnola

TOMATO SAUCE, MOZZARELLA, MUSHROOMS, FRESH TOMATO, ONION, OREGANO

Makes two 8-inch pan pizzas

A SIMPLE HOMEY PAN-STYLE PIZZA made with readily available ingredients. Served out of the pan, this pizza has an earthy, rustic look, perfect for an informal meal or picnic.

1 recipe Pizza Dough (see page 18), divided into 2 balls and allowed to rise

½ cup Uncooked Tomato Sauce for Pizza (see page 220)

6 ounces mozzarella cheese, sliced ¼ inch thick

10 mushrooms, trimmed, wiped clean, and sliced ¼ inch thick

2 ripe round tomatoes or 4 ripe Roma tomatoes, stem ends removed, halved, and cut into ¼-inch-thick slices

4 thin slices onion, separated into rings

2 pinches dried oregano

Extra-virgin olive oil for drizzling

Place a pizza stone or unglazed tiles on the lowest oven rack. Preheat the oven to 500°F.

Place 1 ball of dough on a lightly floured work surface. Sprinkle a little more flour on top of the ball. Using your fingertips, press the ball down into a large flat disk about ¾ inch thick. Lift the dough and lay it over the back of the fist of one hand. Place your other fist underneath the dough so your fists are almost touching. Now gently stretch the dough by moving your fists away from each other; each time you perform this stretching move, rotate the dough. Continue stretching and rotating until the round of dough is about ½ inch thick and measures about 8 inches across. Press the dough into a lightly oiled 8-inch cake pan. Repeat with the remaining dough ball. Then dimple the dough in each pan with your fingertips, pressing firmly and allowing a thicker rim of dough around the edge of each pizza.

Use the back of a spoon to spread half the tomato sauce over the bottom of each pizza. Distribute the mozzarella over the sauce, then scatter the mushrooms evenly over the cheese. Arrange the tomato and onion slices with the remaining tomato sauce over the mushrooms. Finish by sprinkling on the oregano and drizzling with a generous amount of olive oil.

Bake until the crust is golden, 10 to 12 minutes. Remove the pizzas from the oven.

calzone, sfincione, and panzerotti

While a pizza can be seen as an edible plate, the ultimate open-faced treat, filled pizze are more like traditional double-crust pies. In Italy, there are many regional variations on this theme of a pizza filling enclosed by two crusts. These dishes are most connected with the south of Italy, although they can be found all over the peninsula, often under the name Pizza Rustica.

Many regions have different names for the same food, which can be confusing. Sfincione are the famous double-decker pizze from Sicily. Calzone are filled pizze that are made with a single crust folded in half, looking to some like a trouser leg—hence the name. They can be either baked or deep fried. Panzerotti are little calzone that are fried into tasty golden puffs.

Whatever their name, these "pies" manage to be super-rustic and impressive at the same time. The stretched doughs, once baked, become a landscape of earthy color and satisfying texture, all the more exciting for the surprises contained inside. Once you have made a few of the following recipes, feel free to substitute any of the other doughs in them, including the focaccia dough, to achieve different textures and looks.

Calzone alla Parmigiana

ARTICHOKES, EGGPLANT, SMOKED MOZZARELLA, TOMATO SAUCE

Makes 1 calzone; serves 1

THE RICH INGREDIENTS OF PIZZA ALLA PARMIGIANA find their way into a calzone with delicious results.

4 BABY ARTICHOKES OR, 4 FROZEN ARTICHOKE HEARTS, THAWED AND QUARTERED, OR

1/4 CUP MARINATED ARTICHOKE HEARTS, DRAINED

1/4 CUP OLIVE OIL

1 JAPANESE EGGPLANT, ENDS TRIMMED AND CUT INTO 1/2-INCH DICE

DOUGH FOR ONE 8-INCH PIZZA (SEE PAGE 18), STRETCHED OUT TO A 9-INCH ROUND

3 OUNCES SMOKED MOZZARELLA CHEESE, SLICED 1/4 INCH THICK

2 TABLESPOONS UNCOOKED TOMATO SAUCE FOR PIZZA (SEE PAGE 220)

2 TABLESPOONS GRATED ITALIAN PARMESAN CHEESE

Place a pizza stone or unglazed tiles on the lowest oven rack. Preheat the oven to 475°F.

If using fresh artichokes, remove stems and all coarse outer leaves. Trim any remaining tough dark green bits from the bases. Cook the trimmed artichokes in boiling salted water until the hearts are tender when pierced with the tip of a sharp knife. Drain, let cool, and cut into quarters.

In a medium skillet, heat the olive oil over medium-high heat. Sauté the eggplant, turning to brown evenly, until tender and golden. Drain on paper towels.

Sprinkle some flour onto a wooden pizza peel. Gently lift the stretched dough round onto it. Arrange the smoked mozzarella slices in the center of the half of the dough closest to you. Top the mozzarella with the eggplant and artichokes and then the tomato sauce. Scatter half of the Parmesan cheese over the top. Gently fold the top half of the dough over the filling, gently stretching and adjusting the dough so that the edges meet. Seal the edges by crimping with a fork. Tear a small steam vent in the center of the top.

Shake the wooden peel gently back and forth to make sure the calzone is not stuck to it, then quickly slide the calzone onto the hot baking stone. Bake until the edges are golden and the bottom of the calzone is well browned, about 8 minutes. Using a metal peel or spatula, remove the calzone from the oven. Sprinkle with the remaining Parmesan cheese and serve immediately.

Calzone al Forno

SPINACH, RICOTTA, TOMATO SAUCE, OLIVES, MOZZARELLA

Makes 1 calzone; serves 1 hungry person

FOR A CREAMIER, RICHER CALZONE, we replace the tomato sauce with béchamel sauce, adding it to the ricotta. This variation is particularly delicious as mini-calzone for antipasti.

1/4 BUNCH SPINACH, STEMS TRIMMED AND WELL WASHED

KOSHER SALT TO TASTE

1/2 CUP RICOTTA CHEESE

1/4 CUP UNCOOKED TOMATO SAUCE FOR PIZZA (SEE PAGE 220)

DOUGH FOR ONE 8-INCH PIZZA (SEE PAGE 18), STRETCHED OUT TO A 9-INCH ROUND

5 KALAMATA OR MOROCCAN OIL-CURED OLIVES, PITTED AND HALVED

TWO 1/4-INCH-THICK SLICES MOZZARELLA CHEESE

3 LEAVES FRESH BASIL, COARSELY CHOPPED

1 TEASPOON GRATED ITALIAN PARMESAN CHEESE

Place a pizza stone or unglazed tiles on the lowest oven rack. Preheat the oven to 475°F.

Put the spinach in a saucepan with just the water that clings to the leaves and add salt to taste. Cover and cook over low heat until tender, then drain well in a colander. When the spinach is cool enough to handle, squeeze dry and coarsely chop. Set aside.

In a small bowl, beat together the ricotta and 3 tablespoons of the tomato sauce.

Sprinkle some flour onto a wooden pizza peel. Gently lift the stretched dough round onto it. Mound the ricotta mixture in the center of the half of the dough closest to you. Press the spinach gently onto the ricotta, then press the olives into the filling. Gently fold the top half of the dough over the filling, gently stretching and adjusting the dough so that the edges meet. Seal the edges by crimping with a fork. Tear a small steam vent in the center of the top, and spoon the remaining tomato sauce over the vent. Place a slice of mozzarella on either side of the steam vent.

Shake the wooden peel gently back and forth to make sure the calzone is not stuck to it, then quickly slide the calzone onto the hot baking stone. Bake until the edges are golden and the bottom of the calzone is well browned, about 8 minutes. Using a metal peel or spatula, remove the calzone from the oven. Sprinkle with the basil and Parmesan cheese and serve immediately.

Calzone Fritto

RICOTTA, MOZZARELLA, SALAMI, TOMATO SAUCE

Makes eight 4½-inch calzone

AT THE CAFFÈ WE MAKE THESE FRIED CALZONE the same size as our baked calzone, but we also have the luxury of a large deep fryer. It is easier in a home kitchen to make half-sized calzone. I am tickled every time a calzone fritto leaves the kitchen, for they always look like a giant smile on a plate. Incredibly decadent, they taste like a delicate savory doughnut. Try them even quarter-size as appetizers for your next informal gathering. The amount of filling may seem frugal for this calzone, but it is a necessity: To keep the delicate dough from breaking open during frying, the filling must not be too abundant or too wet. The filling for this recipe will fill eight half-sized calzone, but use any of the fillings for stuffed pizze, remembering to adjust the ingredients so that the filling isn't too wet.

VEGETABLE OIL FOR DEEP-FRYING

1 RECIPE PIZZA DOUGH (SEE PAGE 18), SHAPED INTO 8 BALLS AND ALLOWED TO RISE

1⅓ CUPS RICOTTA CHEESE, DRAINED

8 OUNCES MOZZARELLA CHEESE, SLICED ¼ INCH THICK

24 THIN SLICES SALAMI (OPTIONAL)

½ CUP UNCOOKED TOMATO SAUCE FOR PIZZA (SEE PAGE 220)

In a large heavy saucepan or a deep-fat fryer, heat the oil to 375°F. Press and stretch each dough ball out to a 5-inch round, following the directions on page 19.

Sprinkle some flour onto a wooden pizza peel or floured baking sheet. Gently lift the first stretched dough round onto it. Spread about 1 tablespoon ricotta over the pizza round, placing it on the half of the pizza round closest to you and leaving a generous border of dough. Top with a few slices of mozzarella, and 3 slices salami if desired. Spoon 1 tablespoon of the tomato sauce over the filling and gently fold the top half of the dough round over the filling, gently stretching the dough so that the edges meet. Seal the edges by firmly crimping and pinching them to prevent the filling from leaking out into the hot oil. Repeat the process with the remaining dough balls. Gently lift the calzone off the peel, in batches, and slide them into the hot oil. Cook until golden, turning once, then use a slotted spoon to remove them from the oil and drain briefly on paper towels. Serve immediately.

Pizza Maradona

RICOTTA, MOZZARELLA, SALAMI, PROSCIUTTO, TOMATO SAUCE

Makes one 8-inch stuffed pizza

NAMED FOR THE ITALIAN SOCCER PLAYER MARADONA, presumably because his exploits are so legendary, he must require this much food as fuel to keep him going.

DOUGH FOR TWO 8-INCH PIZZAS (SEE PAGE 18), EACH STRETCHED OUT TO A 9-INCH ROUND

$1/2$ CUP RICOTTA CHEESE, DRAINED IF RUNNY

4 OUNCES MOZZARELLA CHEESE, SLICED $1/4$ INCH THICK

2 SLICES SALAMI, TORN INTO BITE-SIZED PIECES (OPTIONAL)

2 SLICES PROSCIUTTO, TORN INTO BITE-SIZED PIECES (OPTIONAL)

12 LEAVES FRESH BASIL, COARSELY CHOPPED

$1/4$ CUP UNCOOKED TOMATO SAUCE FOR PIZZA (SEE PAGE 220)

1 TABLESPOON GRATED ITALIAN PARMESAN CHEESE

Place a pizza stone or unglazed tiles on the lowest oven rack. Preheat the oven to 500°F.

Sprinkle some flour onto a wooden pizza peel. Gently lift one of the stretched pizza circles onto it. Dollop the ricotta over the pizza, leaving a $1/2$-inch border all around. Distribute half the sliced mozzarella evenly over the ricotta. If desired, scatter the salami and prosciutto over the cheeses. Scatter half the basil over the top.

Lay the second pizza dough circle over the top, stretching it gently so that the edges of the two rounds of dough meet. Press and crimp the edges together firmly. Using the back of a spoon, spread the tomato sauce over the top of the pizza. Top with the remaining basil, mozzarella, and Parmesan cheese.

Shake the wooden peel gently back and forth to make sure the pizza is not stuck to it, then quickly slide the pizza onto the hot baking stone. Bake until the pizza edges are golden and the bottom is well browned, about 10 minutes. Using a metal peel or spatula, remove the pizza from the oven.

Pizza Rustica

RICOTTA, MORTADELLA, AGED PROVOLONE

Makes one 8-inch stuffed pizza

A TRADITIONAL SOUTHERN ITALIAN DOUBLE-CRUSTED PIZZA filled with humble, easy-to-find ingredients. Aged provolone is the table version of the softer sandwich cheese. It has a texture similar to string cheese and a sweet, salty bite, perfect for savory pies. Adding a beaten egg white to the cheese and mortadella gives the filling an unusual lightness.

$1/2$ CUP RICOTTA CHEESE, DRAINED

1 TABLESPOON GRATED ITALIAN PARMESAN CHEESE

2 THIN SLICES MORTADELLA, TORN INTO BITE-SIZED PIECES

2 OUNCES AGED PROVOLONE CHEESE, COARSELY CHOPPED

1 LARGE EGG WHITE, BEATEN UNTIL FROTHY

DOUGH FOR TWO 8-INCH PIZZAS (SEE PAGE 18), EACH STRETCHED OUT TO A 9-INCH ROUND

2 GARLIC CLOVES, PEELED AND THINLY SLICED

1 SPRIG ROSEMARY, LEAVES ONLY, FINELY CHOPPED

Place a pizza stone or unglazed tiles on the lowest oven rack. Preheat the oven to 500°F.

In a medium bowl, combine the ricotta, Parmesan, mortadella, and provolone with the egg white and toss together gently until well mixed. Set aside.

Sprinkle some flour onto a wooden pizza peel and gently lift one of the stretched dough rounds onto it. Spread the ricotta mixture over the pizza base, leaving a $1/2$-inch border all around. Lay the other dough round over the top, stretching it gently so that the edges of the two rounds meet. Press and crimp the edges together firmly. Tear 3 to 4 small vents in the top layer of dough to allow the steam to escape. Scatter the garlic and rosemary over the top of the pizza, pressing lightly so the herbs remain in place.

Shake the wooden peel gently back and forth to make sure the pizza is not stuck to it, then quickly slide the pizza onto the hot baking stone. Bake until the pizza edges are golden and the bottom is well browned, about 10 minutes. Using a metal peel or spatula, remove the pizza from the oven.

Sfincione alla Trapanese

FRESH TUNA, HERBS, CAPERS, TOMATO-BASIL SAUCE

Makes one 9-inch sfincione

SFINCIONE ARE SICILIAN PIZZA PIES. The pizza dough, top and bottom, completely encloses the filling to create a beautiful, super-rustic, portable treat. This version from the town of Trapani is one of my favorites.

1 SMALL ONION, PEELED, CUT IN HALF, AND THINLY SLICED

$1/4$ CUP EXTRA-VIRGIN OLIVE OIL

2 GARLIC CLOVES, PEELED AND MINCED

$1^1/2$ POUNDS FRESH TUNA, COARSELY CHOPPED

$1^1/4$ CUPS TOMATO-BASIL SAUCE (SEE PAGE 221)

SMALL HANDFUL OF COARSELY CHOPPED FRESH ITALIAN PARSLEY

6 FRESH BASIL LEAVES, COARSELY CHOPPED

$1/4$ CUP PITTED KALAMATA OR GAETA OLIVES

1 TABLESPOON CAPERS

KOSHER SALT AND FRESHLY GROUND BLACK PEPPER TO TASTE

JUICE OF $1/2$ LEMON

1 RECIPE PIZZA DOUGH (SEE PAGE 18) OR SEMOLINA DOUGH (SEE PAGE 80), SHAPED INTO 2 BALLS AND ALLOWED TO RISE

1 CUP GARLICKY BREAD CRUMBS (SEE PAGE 228) OR COARSE DRY BREAD CRUMBS

2 TABLESPOONS GRATED ITALIAN PARMESAN CHEESE

In a large sauté pan, sauté the onion in the olive oil, until just beginning to soften. Add the garlic and tuna and cook over medium heat, stirring, until the tuna just loses its pink color. Add 1 cup of the tomato sauce, the parsley, basil, olives, capers, and salt and pepper and cook until the tuna is completely cooked. Add the lemon juice. Transfer to a bowl and set aside to cool to room temperature. (This mixture can be made up to 3 days ahead and refrigerated.)

Place a pizza stone or unglazed tiles on the lowest rack of the oven and preheat the oven to 500°F.

On a lightly floured surface, roll out each piece of dough into a circle 9 inches in diameter (or stretch it out following the directions on page 19). Sprinkle some flour onto a wooden pizza peel and gently lift one of the dough circles onto it. Sprinkle half of the bread crumbs evenly over the dough, leaving a ½-inch border, then top with the tuna mixture. Finish by sprinkling the remaining bread crumbs over the tuna. Lay the other dough circle over the top, gently stretching and adjusting it so that the edges of the two dough circles meet. Press and crimp the edges together firmly. Tear 3 small steam vents in the top of the pizza dough.

Spoon the remaining ¼ cup tomato sauce over the sfincione, spreading it over the uneven top with the back of a spoon, and sprinkle the Parmesan cheese over the top. Shake the wooden peel gently back and forth to make sure the sfincione is not stuck to it, then quickly slide it onto the hot baking stone. Bake until the edges are golden and the bottom is light brown, about 12 minutes. Using a metal peel or spatula, remove the sfincione from the oven.

Sfincione Palermitano

ONIONS, ANCHOVIES, OLIVES, TOMATO SAUCE, PARMESAN

Makes one 9-inch sfincione

THE CLASSIC SICILIAN PIZZA PIE, created by the sisters of the convent of San Vito in Palermo.

2 MEDIUM ONIONS, PEELED, HALVED LENGTHWISE, AND SLICED

1 TABLESPOON EXTRA-VIRGIN OLIVE OIL

1 RECIPE SEMOLINA DOUGH (SEE PAGE 80), SHAPED INTO 2 BALLS AND ALLOWED TO RISE

1/2 CUP GARLICKY BREAD CRUMBS (SEE PAGE 228)

4 ANCHOVIES (OR TO TASTE), FINELY CHOPPED

6 MOROCCAN OR OTHER OIL-CURED BLACK OLIVES, PITTED AND HALVED

2 TABLESPOONS UNCOOKED TOMATO SAUCE FOR PIZZA (SEE PAGE 220)

1 TABLESPOON GRATED ITALIAN PARMESAN CHEESE

In a medium skillet, sauté the onions in the olive oil until they are golden and limp. Set aside to cool completely. Place a pizza stone or unglazed tiles on the lowest oven rack and preheat the oven to 500°F.

On a lightly floured surface, roll out each piece of dough into a circle 9 inches in diameter (or stretch it out following the directions on page 19). Sprinkle some flour onto a wooden pizza peel, and gently lift one of the rolled dough rounds onto it. Sprinkle half of the bread crumbs evenly over the dough, leaving a 1/2-inch border all around. Top with the chopped anchovies and the olives, then mound the onions in an even layer over the top. Finish by sprinkling with the remaining bread crumbs. Lay the other dough round over the top, gently stretching and adjusting it so that the edges of the two rounds meet. Press and crimp the edges together firmly. Tear 4 small vents in the dough to allow the steam to escape. Spoon the tomato sauce onto the sfincione, spreading it over the uneven top with the back of a spoon, and sprinkle the Parmesan cheese over the top.

Shake the wooden peel gently back and forth to make sure the sfincione is not stuck to it, then quickly slide the sfincione onto the hot baking stone. Bake until the edges of the sfincione are golden and the bottom is well browned, about 12 minutes. Using a metal peel or spatula, remove the sfincione from the oven.

Panzerotti

RICOTTA, SALAMI, TOMATO SAUCE

Makes 12 panzerotti

THESE LOVELY LITTLE FRIED PUFFS FILLED WITH a savory mixture of ricotta, salami, and tomato sauce are perfect for cocktails. Don't be tempted to add extra tomato sauce. If the filling is too moist, the puffs will break open during frying.

1 RECIPE PIZZA DOUGH (SEE PAGE 18), ALLOWED TO RISE ONCE

3/4 CUP RICOTTA CHEESE, PROCESSED FOR 30 SECONDS IN A FOOD PROCESSOR, OR JUST UNTIL CREAMY

6 THIN SLICES SALAMI, TORN INTO SMALL BITE-SIZED PIECES

ABOUT 1/2 CUP UNCOOKED TOMATO SAUCE FOR PIZZA (SEE PAGE 220)

VEGETABLE OIL FOR DEEP FRYING

1/4 CUP GRATED ITALIAN PARMESAN CHEESE (OPTIONAL)

Sprinkle a work surface with flour. Punch the dough down and turn it out onto the work surface. Divide the dough in half and set aside one half, covering it with a towel. Roll out the remaining dough into a large rectangle about 10 inches by 15 inches and about 1/4 inch thick. Cut the rectangle into six 5-inch squares.

Spoon 1 tablespoon of the creamed ricotta into the center of each square, leaving a generous border of dough. Top the ricotta with a few pieces of salami and press down lightly to compact the filling. Spoon 1 to 2 teaspoons of tomato sauce over the filling. Fold the squares in half so that the edges meet (the panzerotti will measure approximately 5 inches by 2½ inches). Seal the edges by firmly crimping and pinching them so that the filling will not leak out into the cooking oil. Repeat this process with the remaining dough.

In a large heavy saucepan or a deep-fat fryer, heat the vegetable oil to 375°F. Fry the panzerotti in batches, turning frequently to ensure even cooking, until they are golden brown all over. Remove from the oil with a slotted spoon and drain briefly on paper towels. Sprinkle with a little Parmesan cheese if desired and serve warm on a plate lined with paper napkins.

Panzerotti Dolci

SWEETENED RICOTTA, CANDIED CITRUS PEEL

Makes approximately 20 panzerotti

WHENEVER I MAKE THIS DESSERT VERSION of panzerotti, they disappear as fast as I can spoon them from the bubbling oil.

1 CUP PLUS 1 TABLESPOON RICOTTA CHEESE

3/4 CUP SUGAR

1/4 CUP CANDIED CITRUS PEEL (SEE PAGE 229)

1 RECIPE PIZZA DOUGH (SEE PAGE 18), ALLOWED TO RISE 1 HOUR

VEGETABLE OIL FOR DEEP FRYING

POWDERED SUGAR FOR DUSTING

In a food processor fitted with the steel blade, combine the ricotta and sugar and pulse until creamy. Using a rubber spatula, transfer to a mixing bowl and fold in the candied citrus peel.

Sprinkle a work surface with flour. Punch the dough down and turn it out onto the work surface. Divide the dough in half and set aside one half, covering it with a towel. Roll the remaining dough out into a large rectangle about 1/4 inch thick. Using a cookie or biscuit cutter, cut the dough into 3-inch circles.

Spoon 2 teaspoons of the creamed ricotta into the center of each circle, leaving a generous border of dough. Seal the edges by firmly crimping and pinching them so that the filling will not leak out into the cooking oil. Repeat this process with the remaining dough.

Meanwhile, in a large heavy saucepan or a deep-fat fryer, heat the vegetable oil to 375°F. Fry the panzerotti in batches, turning frequently to ensure even cooking, until they are golden brown all over. Remove from the oil with a slotted spoon and drain on paper towels. Use a fine sieve to dust the panzerotti with a little powdered sugar. Serve them warm on a plate lined with paper napkins.

focacce

Focaccia, like pizza, is made in many different thicknesses and textures. The most rustic are irregular flat rectangles that bake into variegated brown sheets with crunchy exteriors and a sturdy interior crumb. At Angeli, we usually make focacce that are closer to a seasoned bread than a pizza. They are one to two inches high and their texture is nearly cakelike, with a moist, evenly textured crumb. The result is well suited for panini or for snacking on its own.

The seasonings or flavorings can be worked directly into the dough or placed atop it like a pizza. The dough can also be used for any of the filled pizze, for a more delicate pie. The examples here range from the simplest, best served as an accompaniment to meals, to the more rich and complex, wonderful as a light snack or lunch with salad or split in half and used for making panini.

note on baking focaccia

Focaccia dough is nearly always placed in a baking pan or on a baking sheet before it is put into the oven, so it isn't necessary to use pizza stones. If you have tiles as a more or less permanent fixture in your oven, set the baking pan directly onto them. The intensity of the heat in the tiles will give the resultant focaccia more character.

Most of the recipes in this section are written to make one large focaccia, but they can also be shaped into several smaller rounds. Follow the technique for Focaccia con Olive e Formaggio on page 73 to make mini-versions.

Focaccia Dough

Makes enough for one 9 by 12-inch focaccia

THERE ARE SEVERAL WAYS TO WORK additional flavorings, such as olives, pancetta, capers, or herbs, into this basic dough. You can spread the flavoring on a floured work surface, turn out the dough on top of it, and gently work it into the dough. Or add the ingredients to the flour in the bowl of the food processor when you make the dough; adding ingredients this way usually results in a more intense flavor and a more uniform color in the dough. This uniformity, however, is not always better, so be sure you want that kind of look and taste before using this method to add tasty bits to your dough.

1 PACKAGE (1 SCANT TABLESPOON) ACTIVE DRY YEAST

½ CUP WARM WATER

1 CUP PLUS 2 TABLESPOONS ROOM-TEMPERATURE WATER

3 TABLESPOONS OLIVE OIL

3 CUPS UNBLEACHED ALL-PURPOSE FLOUR, PLUS ¼ CUP FOR KNEADING

2 TEASPOONS SALT

To make the dough by hand

In a large mixing bowl, stir the yeast into the warm water; let stand until creamy, about 10 minutes. Stir in the room-temperature water and the oil. Add 1 cup of the flour and the salt and whisk or stir until smooth. If you are adding any flavoring ingredients to the dough, add them now. Stir in 2 more cups, then knead in up to ¼ cup more, until the dough comes together. Turn the dough out onto a floured surface and knead until velvety and soft, 8 to 10 minutes.

To make the dough in a food processor

In a small bowl, stir the yeast into the warm water, and let stand until creamy, about 10 minutes. Place the 3 cups flour and the salt in a food processor with the metal blade and pulse 2 or 3 times to sift it. If you are adding any flavoring ingredients, add them now. With the machine running, pour the room-temperature water, the dissolved yeast, and the oil through the feed tube and process until the dough gathers into a rough mass. Process 20 seconds longer to knead. Turn the dough out onto a floured surface and knead by hand, gradually adding the additional ¼ cup of flour, until the dough is velvety and elastic, 2 to 3 minutes.

Place the dough in a lightly oiled bowl, turn once to coat, and cover with plastic wrap or a kitchen towel. Let rise until doubled, about 1½ hours.

Lightly oil a 9 by 12-inch baking pan. Turn the dough out of the bowl into the pan. Gently begin to stretch the dough into a rectangle without crushing all the air bubbles out of it; stretch the dough from the center outward to get an even thickness. Because the gluten that creates the elasticity in the dough is very active, you may not be able to get the dough to stay in the corners—it will want to snap back toward the center. If so, just set the pan aside, covered, for 10 minutes; the gluten should relax enough to enable you to coax the dough into the corners of the pan. Firmly press the dough into the corners and then press it gently into an even thickness over all. Cover the dough with a towel and let rise for 30 minutes.

Dimple the dough all over with your fingertips, leaving indentations that are about ½ inch deep. Cover the dough with a moist towel and let rise until doubled, about 1½ hours.

The focaccia is now ready to top and bake.

Focaccia al Rosmarino

ROSEMARY, COARSE SALT

Makes one 9 by 12-inch focaccia

THERE IS ALMOST NO LIMIT to the amount of oil you can drizzle on a focaccia. The more you use before it is baked, the more flavor and crunch the top crust will have. If you prefer a tender crust, simply brush a bit of olive oil over the top when the focaccia comes out of the oven.

> ONE 9 BY 12-INCH PAN FOCACCIA DOUGH (SEE PAGE 68), ALLOWED TO RISE
>
> 2 TEASPOONS FINELY CHOPPED FRESH ROSEMARY
>
> KOSHER SALT FOR SPRINKLING
>
> EXTRA-VIRGIN OLIVE OIL FOR DRIZZLING

Preheat the oven to 425°F.

Again dimple the surface of the focaccia with your fingertips, creating lots of little indentations to catch the flavorings. Sprinkle the rosemary and salt over the dough and drizzle generously with olive oil. Place the pan in the oven and bake 30 to 35 minutes, or until golden on top. Serve warm or at room temperature.

Focaccia Sfincione

ONION, SAGE, BREAD CRUMBS, PECORINO ROMANO

Makes one 9 by 12-inch focaccia

SOME OF THE TRADITIONAL INGREDIENTS OF Sicily's famed sfincione are placed atop focaccia dough for an especially savory treat.

½ SMALL ONION, THINLY SLICED

1 TABLESPOON EXTRA-VIRGIN OLIVE OIL

4 LARGE FRESH SAGE LEAVES, COARSELY CHOPPED

ONE 9 BY 12-INCH PAN FOCACCIA DOUGH (SEE PAGE 68), ALLOWED TO RISE

¼ CUP GARLICKY BREAD CRUMBS (SEE PAGE 228) OR PLAIN DRY BREAD CRUMBS

½ CUP GRATED IMPORTED PECORINO ROMANO CHEESE

EXTRA-VIRGIN OLIVE OIL FOR DRIZZLING

Preheat the oven to 425°F.

In a small skillet, cook the onion in the olive oil over low heat until limp and almost translucent. Remove from the heat and let cool.

Scatter the onion and sage over the dough. Sprinkle on the bread crumbs and grated cheese and drizzle generously with olive oil. Place the pan in the oven and bake 30 to 35 minutes, or until golden on top. Serve warm or at room temperature.

Focaccia all'Uovo

EGG, CREAM, PARMESAN

Makes one 9 by 12-inch focaccia

ONE OF THE SIMPLEST OF FOCACCE. Egg and cream are beaten together and drizzled over the risen dough to bake to a rich, savory finish. Perfect for panini or for breakfast with a steaming cup of caffè latte. For extra richness, beat a couple of tablespoons of mascarpone into the mixture.

> 2 LARGE EGGS BEATEN WITH $\frac{1}{4}$ CUP HEAVY CREAM
>
> ONE 9 BY 12-INCH PAN FOCACCIA DOUGH (SEE PAGE 68), ALLOWED TO RISE
>
> 1 TABLESPOON GRATED ITALIAN PARMESAN CHEESE

Preheat the oven to 425°F.

Drizzle the egg and cream mixture evenly over the dough and sprinkle with the Parmesan cheese. Place the pan in the oven and bake 30 to 35 minutes, or until golden on top. Serve warm or at room temperature.

Focaccia Ricca

MASCARPONE, PARMESAN

Makes one 9 by 12-inch focaccia

ANOTHER RICH BUT SIMPLE DISH. Delicious as an appetizer cut into thin fingers and served with a velvety red wine.

> 1 TO 2 CUPS MASCARPONE CHEESE (TO TASTE)
>
> ONE 9 BY 12-INCH PAN FOCACCIA DOUGH (SEE PAGE 68), ALLOWED TO RISE
>
> $\frac{1}{4}$ CUP GRATED ITALIAN PARMESAN CHEESE

Preheat the oven to 425°F.

Place tablespoon-sized dollops of mascarpone evenly over the dough. Sprinkle all over with the Parmesan cheese. Place the pan in the oven and bake 30 to 35 minutes, or until golden on top. Serve warm or at room temperature.

Focaccia alla Scarola

ESCAROLE, ONION, ANCHOVY, OLIVES, CAPERS, PINE NUTS, RAISINS

Makes one 9 by 12-inch focaccia

ESCAROLE IS ONE OF MY FAVORITE VEGETABLES. This traditional topping combines its tender bitter-sweetness with the salty punch of anchovy, olives, and capers. Raisins add sweetness and pine nuts round out the flavor. Delicious served on a picnic, accompanied by some creamy Teleme cheese and spicy Italian country salami.

$1/4$ HEAD ESCAROLE, CORE REMOVED

2 TABLESPOONS EXTRA-VIRGIN OLIVE OIL

$1/2$ SMALL ONION, PEELED AND THINLY SLICED

KOSHER SALT TO TASTE

1 ANCHOVY FILLET, COARSELY CHOPPED (OPTIONAL)

10 KALAMATA OR MOROCCAN OIL-CURED OLIVES, PITTED AND HALVED

ONE 9 BY 12-INCH PAN FOCACCIA DOUGH (SEE PAGE 68), ALLOWED TO RISE

1 TABLESPOON CAPERS, DRAINED

1 TABLESPOON PINE NUTS

1 TABLESPOON GOLDEN RAISINS, PLUMPED FOR 15 MINUTES IN HOT WATER, THEN DRAINED (OPTIONAL)

EXTRA-VIRGIN OLIVE OIL FOR DRIZZLING

Preheat the oven to 425°F.

Blanch the escarole in a large pot of boiling salted water for 1 minute; drain. When the escarole is cool enough to handle, squeeze dry and chop very coarsely.

Heat the olive oil in a small sauté pan. Add the onion and cook over low heat until very soft and barely golden in color. Season with salt to taste and remove from the heat.

Distribute the anchovy if desired, the escarole, and olives over the focaccia. Sprinkle with the capers, pine nuts, and the raisins, if desired. Drizzle with olive oil. Place the pan in the oven and bake 30 to 35 minutes, or until golden on top. Serve warm or at room temperature.

Focaccia con Olive e Formaggio

OLIVE PASTE, PROSCIUTTO, FONTINA

Makes three 8-inch-round focacce

THE OLIVE PASTE IS ADDED TO THE DOUGH ITSELF so that it creates marbleized pockets throughout the finished focaccia. It is finished off with the rich sweetness of prosciutto and Fontina cheese.

1/4 CUP BLACK OLIVE PASTE

1 RECIPE FOCACCIA DOUGH (SEE PAGE 68), KNEADED BUT NOT RISEN

2 THIN SLICES PROSCIUTTO, TORN INTO SMALL BITE-SIZED PIECES

2 THIN SLICES ITALIAN FONTINA CHEESE (ABOUT 2 OUNCES), TORN INTO SMALL
BITE-SIZED PIECES

EXTRA-VIRGIN OLIVE OIL FOR DRIZZLING

Preheat the oven to 425°F.

Knead the olive paste into the focaccia dough just until it is marbleized throughout the dough but not uniformly mixed through. Place the dough in a lightly oiled bowl, turn once to coat, and cover with plastic wrap or a kitchen towel. Let rise until doubled, about 1½ hours.

Divide the dough into 3 equal pieces. Place each piece in a lightly oiled 8-inch cake pan lined with parchment paper and pat out to an even thickness. Dimple the dough deeply with your fingertips, then scatter the prosciutto and Fontina over the dough. Drizzle olive oil generously over the focacce.

Place the pans in the oven and bake 30 to 35 minutes, or until golden on top. Serve warm or at room temperature.

Focaccia di Marcello

TOMATO, ONION, OLIVES, HERBS

Makes one 9 by 12-inch focaccia

A FORMER PIZZAIÒLO, Marcello is Argentine of Italian descent. This is the focaccia he loved most to make for his family—and the Angeli family when he was feeling particularly paternal. A very light version of pan pizza, this savory treat stands on its own for a casual family supper, accompanied by just a simple salad.

1 ROMA TOMATO, STEM END REMOVED AND THINLY SLICED

ONE 9 BY 12-INCH PAN FOCACCIA DOUGH (SEE PAGE 68), ALLOWED TO RISE

2 THIN SLICES ONION, SEPARATED INTO RINGS

5 KALAMATA OR MOROCCAN OIL-CURED OLIVES, PITTED AND HALVED

1 SMALL SPRIG ROSEMARY, LEAVES ONLY, FINELY CHOPPED

1/2 TEASPOON DRIED OREGANO

EXTRA-VIRGIN OLIVE OIL FOR DRIZZLING

Preheat the oven to 425°F.

Lay the tomato slices evenly on the dough. Scatter the onion and olives over the tomatoes. Sprinkle the rosemary and oregano over all and finish with a generous drizzle of olive oil. Place the pan in the oven and bake 30 to 35 minutes, or until golden on top. Serve warm or at room temperature.

Schiacciata all'Uva

Makes one 11 by 17-inch schiacciata

THE WORD *SCHIACCIATA* MEANS "CRUSHED," and it refers in this instance to the very flat nature of this type of focaccia. The dough used for schiacciata is our basic focaccia dough, but it is baked as a much larger rectangle.

Schiacciata was originally prepared as a snack for the workers during the autumnal grape harvest in preparation for making wine. It is therefore most traditional to top schiacciata with wine grapes. In this country, the most readily available wine grapes are Zinfandel or Corinth, but seedless Red Flame is a fine substitute.

3 CUPS RIPE YET FIRM FRAGRANT RED GRAPES

1 CUP MARASCHINO LIQUEUR (OPTIONAL)

1 RECIPE FOCACCIA DOUGH (SEE PAGE 68), ALLOWED TO RISE ONCE

3/4 CUP WALNUTS, CHOPPED

1/3 CUP SUGAR

If desired, put the grapes in a small glass or stainless bowl with the maraschino and let macerate while you prepare the dough.

Turn the risen dough out onto a lightly oiled 11 by 17-inch baking pan and stretch it with your fingertips toward the edges as if you were making focaccia (see page 68); you may need to stretch the dough, let it rest briefly, and then stretch some more. Push the dough with your fingertips to spread it evenly into the corners.

If you soaked the grapes, lift them out of their juices with a slotted spoon. Evenly distribute the grapes over the dough. Top with the walnuts. Cover with a towel and let the focaccia rise until puffy and doubled, about 1 hour.

Preheat the oven to 400°F.

Sprinkle the top of the focaccia with the sugar. Bake 15 minutes, then turn the oven down to 375°F, and continue baking another 10 to 15 minutes, until golden. After the schiacciata has baked for 20 minutes, tilt the pan to distribute the sugary juices evenly over the top of the bread.

savory tarts and snacks

A savory tart is often the perfect dish to take to a potluck or any casual get-together. Portable and pretty, these tarts are much simpler to prepare than their impressive appearance would indicate.

Here is an assortment of savory tarts, as well as a couple of snacks, a Pugliese bread, and, of course, Angeli pizza bread. The tarts are a natural offshoot of our pizzas. They range from a quichelike shallow tart filled with coarse zucchini puree to the classic layered Italian picnic tart, Torta Rustica. Play around with the doughs until you find which ones suit your taste and time the best, or interchange them to create a personalized version of these dishes.

Pasta Frolla (Flaky Pastry Dough)

Makes enough for a 10-inch tart

A SIMPLE FLAKY PASTRY DOUGH suitable for savory fillings, this can be made in advance and frozen for up to one month. To use, defrost overnight in the refrigerator. Tart shells can also be rolled out in advance and stored, carefully wrapped, in the freezer; prebake while still frozen.

2½ CUPS UNBLEACHED ALL-PURPOSE FLOUR

¼ TEASPOON SALT

8 OUNCES (2 STICKS) COLD UNSALTED BUTTER, CUT INTO PIECES

6 TABLESPOONS ICE WATER

Combine the flour and salt in a bowl. Stir to mix. Add the butter pieces and rapidly cut the butter into the flour with your fingertips or two knives until the mixture resembles coarse meal. Gradually add the water and mix the dough with a fork until it just comes together. Gather the dough into a ball, wrap in plastic wrap, and refrigerate at least 1 hour.

When ready to make a tart, unwrap the dough and place on a lightly floured board. Hit the dough a few times with a rolling pin to soften it. Roll out into a 12-inch round between ⅛ and ¼ inch thick. Gently lift the dough up on the rolling pin and ease into a 10-inch tart pan with a removable bottom. Firmly press the dough into the pan without stretching. Trim the overhang by running the rolling pin over the top of the pan. Refrigerate for at least 30 minutes, or until ready to use.

To partially prebake the shell, preheat the oven to 400°F.

Line the tart shell with aluminum foil. Fill with pie weights, rice, or dried beans. Bake for 15 minutes. Remove from the oven and lift out the aluminum foil and weights. Prick the bottom with a fork. Bake another 3 to 5 minutes, until the pastry looks dry. Let cool.

Pasta Morbida (Soft Tart Dough)

Makes enough for a 14-inch double-crusted tart

AN EXTREMELY FORGIVING SOFT DOUGH that is wonderful to use when you're in a hurry—or when cooking with children. For easier handling, roll out the dough on parchment, wax paper, aluminum foil, or plastic wrap. Its rustic charm is particularly suited to decorated double-crusted tarts.

4 CUPS UNBLEACHED ALL-PURPOSE FLOUR

1 TEASPOON SALT

8 OUNCES (2 STICKS) COLD UNSALTED BUTTER, CUT INTO PIECES

2 LARGE EGGS

2 EGG YOLKS

1/3 CUP MILK (APPROXIMATELY)

To make the dough by hand

Combine the flour and salt in a large bowl. Make a well in the center and add the butter, eggs, and yolks. Lightly blend the butter mixture with your fingertips. With a knife or pastry blender, cut the wet ingredients into the dry ingredients until the dough is crumbly. Gradually add just enough milk, tossing with a fork, so the dough comes together; the dough will be soft. Gather the dough into a ball. Wrap dough in plastic wrap and refrigerate for at least 1 hour, or up to 2 or 3 days.

To make the dough in a food processor

Combine the flour, salt, and butter in a food processor fitted with the metal blade. Process with short pulses until the mixture is crumbly. Add the eggs and yolks and pulse just to blend; do not overmix. Gradually add just enough milk, pulsing, so the dough begins to come together. Remove the dough and proceed as directed above.

Pasta del Pane di Semolina (Semolina Dough)

Makes enough for a 10-inch double-crusted tart

MAKING A SPONGE HELPS PRODUCE A light and tender dough when using semolina flour. Since this recipe is really a bread dough, it results in a thick yet light crust whose uniform crumb is perfectly suited to moist fillings.

FOR THE SPONGE

1 PACKAGE (1 SCANT TABLESPOON) ACTIVE DRY YEAST OR $^1/_2$ OUNCE FRESH YEAST, CRUMBLED

$^3/_4$ CUP WARM WATER

$^1/_2$ CUP UNBLEACHED ALL-PURPOSE FLOUR

$^1/_2$ CUP SEMOLINA FLOUR

TO COMPLETE THE DOUGH

$^1/_4$ CUP WATER

$^1/_4$ CUP EXTRA-VIRGIN OLIVE OIL

$^1/_2$ TEASPOON SALT

$^1/_2$ CUP UNBLEACHED ALL-PURPOSE FLOUR

$1^1/_4$ TO $1^1/_2$ CUPS SEMOLINA FLOUR, OR MORE IF NECESSARY

To make the sponge, in a small bowl, sprinkle the yeast over the warm water. Let it fizz for about 5 minutes.

In a large bowl, combine the two flours and the yeast mixture. Stir or whisk until you have a thick batter.

Stir the water, oil, and salt into the sponge until smooth. Add the all-purpose flour and $^3/_4$ cup of the semolina flour and stir the mixture with a wooden spoon until it comes together into a rough dough.

Sprinkle a work surface with a little flour, and transfer the dough to the floured surface. Knead in another $^1/_2$ cup semolina flour, a little at a time, kneading for a total of 8 to 10 minutes. The dough should be soft and elastic but not sticky. You may need a little less or a little more flour. Shape the dough into a ball.

Rub the inside of a large mixing bowl with a little cooking oil. Transfer the dough to the bowl, turn once to coat, and cover tightly with plastic wrap. Let the dough rise in a warm place for about 1 hour, or until doubled in bulk.

Sprinkle a work surface with flour. Punch the dough down and divide it in half. Roll each piece into a tight smooth ball, kneading it to push the air out of it. Place the dough balls on a lightly floured surface, cover them with a clean kitchen towel, and let rest for 1 hour. (Or place them on a floured towel on a cookie sheet, cover with a towel, and refrigerate overnight. The dough will keep in the refrigerator for approximately 2 days or in the freezer for up to 1 month; thaw overnight in the refrigerator before using.)

Place 1 of the balls of dough on a lightly floured work surface. Sprinkle a little more flour on top of the ball. Using your fingertips, press the ball down into a large flat disk about ½ inch thick. Lift the dough and lay it over the back of the fist of one hand. Place your other fist underneath the dough so your fists are almost touching. Now gently stretch the dough by moving your fists away from each other; each time you perform this stretching move, rotate the dough. Continue stretching and rotating until the round of dough is about ¼ inch thick and measures about 9 inches across. The dough is now ready for whichever topping you choose. Repeat with the remaining dough ball.

Torta di Ricotta e Spinaci

ONION, SPINACH, RICOTTA, GARLIC

Makes one 10-inch tart

IN ITALY, HOME COOKS USE COOKED SPINACH SO OFTEN in their recipes that you can buy a little centrifuge for whisking away the excess liquid. Since this amazing convenience has not yet hit our shores, there are a few other methods to wring out the spinach. You can wrap the spinach in cheesecloth or a dishcloth and wring the liquid out. You can simply take meatball-sized handfuls of spinach between your palms and press with all your strength. Or (my preferred method) you can place the cooked spinach in a strainer, set the strainer over a bowl, and push down on the spinach.

2 TABLESPOONS EXTRA-VIRGIN OLIVE OIL

1 SMALL ONION, PEELED AND MINCED

1 BUNCH SPINACH, STEMS TRIMMED AND WELL WASHED

1 CUP RICOTTA CHEESE

1 GARLIC CLOVE, PEELED AND MINCED

1/2 CUP GRATED ITALIAN PARMESAN CHEESE

4 LARGE EGGS, BEATEN

1 CUP MILK

KOSHER SALT AND FRESHLY GROUND BLACK PEPPER TO TASTE

1 UNBAKED 10-INCH PASTA FROLLA TART SHELL (SEE PAGE 78)

Preheat the oven to 375°F. Heat the olive oil in a small sauté pan. Add the minced onion and cook over low heat until completely wilted and soft. Set aside to cool.

Put the spinach in a saucepan with just the water that clings to the leaves, cover, and cook over low heat just until it wilts. Drain well and set aside until cool enough to handle, then press all the excess liquid out of the spinach. Coarsely chop the spinach and squeeze dry.

In a medium mixing bowl, beat together the spinach, ricotta, garlic, Parmesan cheese, eggs, and milk. Add the cooled onion and stir to mix well. Season to taste.

Pour the mixture into the tart shell and bake for 30 minutes, or until the blade of a thin knife comes out clean when inserted in the center of the tart. Let cool for 5 minutes before serving. This tart is also excellent at room temperature.

Torta di Zucchini Sfranta

ZUCCHINI, HERBS, PARMESAN

Makes one 9-inch tart

YEARS AGO, WHEN I FIRST READ Edda Servi Machlin's *The Classic Cuisine of the Italian Jews*,
I became enchanted with her recipe for Zucchini Sfranta, a simple vegetable dish in which zucchini is
cooked with herbs and oil until it completely falls apart into a coarse puree. Over the years this preparation has found its way into many dishes in the Angeli kitchen. It is a natural base for this easy-to-
make savory tart.

2 MEDIUM ZUCCHINI, ENDS TRIMMED AND COARSELY CHOPPED

$1/4$ CUP OLIVE OIL

$1/4$ CUP WATER

1 BUNCH FRESH BASIL, LEAVES ONLY, COARSELY CHOPPED

1 GARLIC CLOVE, PEELED AND MINCED

KOSHER SALT AND FRESHLY GROUND BLACK PEPPER TO TASTE

3 LARGE EGGS

$1/2$ CUP GRATED ITALIAN PARMESAN CHEESE

1 UNBAKED 10-INCH PASTA FROLLA TART SHELL (SEE PAGE 78)

Place the zucchini in a small saucepan and add the olive oil, water, basil, garlic, and salt and pepper to taste. Bring to a simmer, cover, and cook over low heat, stirring occasionally, until the zucchini falls apart and the mixture becomes a coarse puree. Pour into a mixing bowl and set aside to
cool to room temperature.

Preheat the oven to 375°F.

Add the eggs and Parmesan to the cooled zucchini mixture and stir well to mix. Pour the
mixture into the tart shell and bake for about 30 minutes, or until the filling is slightly puffed and
golden and the blade of a thin knife comes out clean when inserted in the center.

Pissaladiera

ONIONS, OREGANO, TOMATOES, GARLICKY BREAD CRUMBS, OLIVES, ANCHOVIES
Makes one 9-inch tart

THE CLASSIC TART OF THE RIVIERA. Iconic Mediterranean ingredients are combined in a simple tart crust to create an exceptionally flavorful dish. Although traditionally served as a merenda, or afternoon snack, this tart works well as a light luncheon dish or for a picnic. We often make a smaller version in three-inch tart pans for cocktail accompaniments.

2 LARGE BERMUDA (YELLOW) ONIONS, PEELED

3 TABLESPOONS EXTRA-VIRGIN OLIVE OIL, PLUS MORE FOR DRIZZLING

2 TEASPOONS DRIED OREGANO

KOSHER SALT AND FRESHLY GROUND BLACK PEPPER TO TASTE

3 FIRM BUT RIPE TOMATOES

1/4 CUP GARLICKY BREAD CRUMBS (SEE PAGE 228)

ONE 10-INCH PASTA FROLLA TART SHELL (SEE PAGE 78), PARTIALLY BAKED

10 TO 15 BRINE-CURED OLIVES, SUCH AS KALAMATA, GAETA, OR NIÇOISE, PITTED

2 TO 3 ANCHOVY FILLETS

Cut the onions in half lengthwise. Lay the halves cut side down and cut into thin crosswise slices.

Heat the olive oil in a large skillet. Add the onions, oregano, and salt and pepper and gently sauté until the onions are translucent and begin to color, 10 to 15 minutes. Turn into a strainer to drain. Remove the stem ends of the tomatoes, cut into 1/2-inch-thick slices, and set on paper towels to drain.

Preheat the oven to 375°F.

To assemble the tart, sprinkle half the bread crumbs over the bottom of the tart shell. Spread the cooked onions evenly over the bread crumbs. Arrange the tomato slices in a concentric circular pattern over the onions. Scatter the olives over the tomatoes. Cut the anchovy fillets in half and arrange them over the tomatoes. Sprinkle the remaining bread crumbs over the tart and drizzle olive oil over all.

Bake for about 20 minutes, or until the onions are hot, the tomatoes are just beginning to dry, and the tart shell is golden brown.

Pasticcio di Caponata

CAPONATA, PARMESAN

Makes one 10-inch double-crusted tart

THE FILLING FOR THIS TART IS VERY SPECIAL. Many of us love the mixture of flavors and textures in a traditional caponata but just can't enjoy the knowledge that just about every ingredient has been fried. Grilling the vegetables is a delicious alternative to frying and it highlights the brilliant colors and characteristic textures of the different ingredients.

FOR THE CAPONATA

2 CELERY STALKS, SLICED

3 GARLIC CLOVES, PEELED AND THINLY SLICED

2 TABLESPOONS EXTRA-VIRGIN OLIVE OIL

2 EGGPLANTS, PEELED, ENDS REMOVED, AND CUT INTO $\frac{1}{4}$-INCH-THICK SLICES

3 ZUCCHINI, TRIMMED AND CUT LENGTHWISE INTO $\frac{1}{4}$-INCH-THICK SLICES

2 CARROTS, PEELED AND CUT LENGTHWISE INTO $\frac{1}{4}$-INCH-THICK SLICES

2 RED BELL PEPPERS, CUT LENGTHWISE IN HALF AND STEMS, SEEDS, AND TOUGH WHITE MEMBRANES REMOVED

1 RED ONION, PEELED AND CUT INTO THICK SLICES

OLIVE OIL FOR BRUSHING

SMALL HANDFUL OF COARSELY CHOPPED FRESH ITALIAN PARSLEY

10 FRESH SAGE LEAVES, FINELY CHOPPED

2 TABLESPOONS CAPERS, DRAINED

$\frac{1}{2}$ CUP PITTED KALAMATA OLIVES

$\frac{1}{2}$ CUP PITTED GREEN OLIVES

$1\frac{1}{2}$ CUPS TOMATO-BASIL SAUCE (SEE PAGE 221) OR CANNED TOMATO SAUCE

$\frac{1}{2}$ CUP VINEGAR, OR TO TASTE

$\frac{1}{4}$ CUP SUGAR, OR TO TASTE

KOSHER SALT AND FRESHLY GROUND BLACK PEPPER TO TASTE

1 LARGE EGG, LIGHTLY BEATEN

1 RECIPE SEMOLINA DOUGH (SEE PAGE 80), DIVIDED INTO 2 PIECES, ONE TWICE AS LARGE AS THE OTHER, AFTER THE FIRST RISE, EACH ONE SHAPED INTO A TIGHT BALL, AND ALLOWED TO REST FOR 1 HOUR

2 TABLESPOONS GRATED ITALIAN PARMESAN CHEESE

To make the caponata, in a medium skillet, sauté the celery and sliced garlic in the oil until the celery is limp and the garlic is barely golden. Transfer to a large mixing bowl and set aside.

Heat a charcoal or gas grill. Grill the eggplants, zucchini, carrots, peppers, and red onion until barely tender, turning occasionally and brushing lightly with olive oil as needed. (Be sure to cook the eggplant until it reaches a creamy texture.) Remove the vegetables with tongs as they finish cooking and set aside to cool.

When the vegetables are cool enough to handle, roughly chop the onion. Cut the remaining vegetables into thin strips. Add the grilled vegetables to the celery-garlic mixture. Add the herbs, capers, olives, and tomato-basil sauce and gently toss to combine. Set aside.

Combine the vinegar and sugar in a small saucepan and heat over low heat until the sugar dissolves. Pour over the vegetables and toss again. Add salt and pepper to taste. Taste for sweet and sour and adjust to taste. Set aside to cool completely before making the tart. (The caponata can be made up to 4 days ahead and refrigerated.)

Preheat the oven to 375°F.

To assemble the tart, add the beaten egg to the caponata and mix well.

Lightly oil a 10-inch springform pan. On a lightly floured surface, roll out the larger of the dough balls into a 13-inch circle. Fit the dough into the pan, tapping it gently into the corners with your fingertips and pushing it up the sides of the pan so that it reaches almost to the top. Spread the caponata in an even layer over the pastry and sprinkle on the Parmesan cheese.

Roll out the smaller dough ball into a 10-inch circle and lay it over the filling. Crimp and pinch the edges until they are well sealed, making a rough and rustic edge (it shouldn't be perfect). Tear or cut 2 small steam vents in the top of the dough.

Bake until the crust is golden and the filling is piping hot, 35 to 40 minutes. Remove from the oven and let cool for 5 minutes. Remove the sides of the springform and place the tart on a serving dish. Serve warm or at room temperature.

Torta Rustica

SPINACH, ONION, ROASTED PEPPERS, CHICKEN, FONTINA
Makes one 14-inch double-crusted tart

THE IDEAL PICNIC FOOD, THIS IMPRESSIVE TART never fails to get rave reviews. When we make the tart for a special occasion, we love to use the leftover scraps of dough to decorate the crust. Grape clusters with stems and leaves seem to be a kitchen favorite. For a great vegetarian entrée, omit the chicken and add a layer of your favorite grilled vegetable instead.

SIX 10-OUNCE PACKAGES FROZEN CHOPPED SPINACH

1 TABLESPOON UNSALTED BUTTER

1 TABLESPOON OLIVE OIL

1 SMALL ONION, MINCED

4 LARGE EGGS

1 CUP GRATED ITALIAN PARMESAN CHEESE

1/2 CUP DRY BREAD CRUMBS

KOSHER SALT AND FRESHLY GROUND PEPPER TO TASTE

4 LARGE RED BELL PEPPERS OR ONE 16-OUNCE JAR GOOD-QUALITY PEELED RED PEPPERS

4 BONELESS SKINLESS CHICKEN BREASTS, POUNDED TO 1/2 INCH THICK

3 TABLESPOONS EXTRA-VIRGIN OLIVE OIL (OPTIONAL)

1 RECIPE SOFT TART DOUGH (SEE PAGE 79)

1/2 POUND ITALIAN FONTINA CHEESE, RIND REMOVED AND SLICED

1 LARGE EGG BEATEN WITH 2 TABLESPOONS MILK, FOR EGG WASH

Cook the spinach according to the package directions. Drain in a colander and rinse under cold water to cool. Drain again and squeeze out the excess moisture with your hands. The spinach should be almost completely dry. Place in a large bowl and set aside.

Heat the butter and oil together in a small skillet. Sauté the minced onion until it becomes translucent and begins to color. And to the spinach. Add the eggs, Parmesan, bread crumbs, and salt and pepper and mix well. Set aside.

If using fresh bell peppers, place them over a gas burner or under a hot broiler and cook, turning with tongs, until they are blackened all over. Place them in a plastic bag, close the top, and let them sweat for 10 minutes. Remove the peppers from the plastic bag and rinse the skins off under cold running water. Lay on paper towels to drain.

Carefully remove the stems from the peppers and slice each one open down one side. Discard the seeds and white ribs. Trim the peppers if necessary so that they will lie flat. Set aside.

Season the chicken with salt and pepper to taste. Cook on a grill, or under a hot broiler; or heat the extra-virgin olive oil in a large skillet and sauté the chicken until just cooked through. When the chicken is cool enough to handle, cut into 1-inch-wide strips. Set aside.

Preheat the oven to 375°F.

To assemble the tart, divide the dough into two pieces, one twice as big as the other.

On parchment, wax paper, aluminum foil, or plastic wrap, roll out the larger piece into a circle approximately 14 inches in diameter. Line the largest mixing bowl you have with plastic wrap. Invert the circle of dough into the bowl. Peel off the paper, making sure the dough lies flat against the sides of the bowl. To layer the ingredients, start with a thin layer of the spinach mixture, then add a layer of red pepper, another of Fontina, and one of chicken strips. Continue layering in any pattern you like, but finish with a layer of spinach at least ½ inch thick. (When you invert the tart for baking, the spinach will be on the bottom.)

Roll out the remaining dough again on parchment, wax paper, aluminum foil, or plastic wrap, into a circle large enough to cover the filling. Invert the dough onto the filling and peel off the paper. Trim the edges of the circle of dough and brush the edges with the egg wash. Fold over the extra dough from the larger dough circle and pinch the edges to seal very well. Carefully invert the tart onto a baking sheet and remove the bowl. Peel off the plastic wrap.

If you would like a sheen to the crust, brush it with the egg wash before placing it in the oven and again once or twice during baking.

Bake the tart for approximately 40 minutes, or until the crust is a deep golden brown. Serve the tart warm or at room temperature, cut into wedges.

'Mpanata alla Catanese (Savory Fresh Tuna Tart)

TUNA, GARLIC, CAULIFLOWER, OLIVES, ANCHOVIES, CHERRY PEPPERS

Makes one 12-inch tart

I HAVE A SPECIAL AFFECTION FOR THIS DISH. It is a beautiful example of how humble ingredients can be combined to create a satisfying, even elegant luncheon or picnic treat. This piquant Sicilian "pizza rustica" comes from the city of Catania and is filled with the strong flavors of the region.

FOR THE FILLING

12 TO 16 OUNCES FRESH TUNA, COARSELY CHOPPED

3 GARLIC CLOVES, PEELED AND SLICED

¼ CUP EXTRA-VIRGIN OLIVE OIL

2 SMALL CAULIFLOWER, TRIMMED AND SEPARATED INTO FLORETS

½ CUP PITTED KALAMATA OR GAETA OLIVES, COARSELY CHOPPED

3 ANCHOVY FILLETS, COARSELY CHOPPED

3 HOT OR SWEET CHERRY PEPPERS, SEEDED AND FINELY CHOPPED (OPTIONAL)

LARGE HANDFUL OF COARSELY CHOPPED FRESH ITALIAN PARSLEY

KOSHER SALT AND FRESHLY GROUND BLACK PEPPER TO TASTE

1 RECIPE SOFT TART DOUGH (SEE PAGE 79)

4 LARGE EGGS, BEATEN

1 LARGE EGG, BEATEN, FOR EGG WASH

To prepare the filling, place the tuna and garlic in a large skillet with the olive oil. Cook over medium heat, stirring frequently, until the tuna is cooked through, 5 to 7 minutes. Transfer the tuna mixture to a large mixing bowl and let cool.

Cook the cauliflower in a large pot of boiling salted water until tender, about 12 minutes. Drain and refresh in a bowl of ice water. Drain again, and add the florets to the tuna.

Add the olives, anchovy fillets, cherry peppers, parsley, and salt and black pepper to taste and mix well. Set aside so the flavors can begin mixing while you roll out the dough. (The filling can be made to this point up to 2 days in advance; cover and refrigerate.)

Preheat the oven to 375°F.

To assemble the tart, divide the dough into two pieces, one twice as large as the other. On parchment paper, wax paper, aluminum foil, or plastic wrap, roll out the larger piece into a circle approximately 14 inches in diameter. Line the largest mixing bowl you have with plastic wrap. Invert the circle of dough into the bowl. Peel off the paper and press the dough against the sides of the bowl.

Stir the eggs into the cauliflower mixture, then place the mixture in the dough-lined bowl.

Roll out the remaining dough as you did the first, into a circle large enough to cover the filling. Invert the dough onto the filling and peel off the paper. Trim the edges of the circle of dough and brush the edges with the egg wash. Fold over the extra dough from the larger dough circle and pinch the edges to seal very well. Carefully invert the tart onto a baking sheet and remove the bowl. Peel off the plastic wrap. If you want a sheen to the crust, brush it with egg wash before placing it in the oven and again once or twice during baking.

Bake the tart for about 40 minutes, or until the crust is a deep golden brown. Serve warm or at room temperature, cut into wedges.

Sfogliata
(Pugliese Bread Seasoned with Sun-Dried Tomato Pesto)

Makes 1 large loaf

SFOGLIATA IS A TRADITIONAL BREAD FROM PUGLIA, the heel of the boot of Italy. The word *sfogliata* means "layered," and in this recipe refers to the fact that the dough is rolled into a rectangle, spread with a savory filling and then rolled up like a jelly roll. Traditionally the roll was then shaped into a large coil. This serpentlike form is typical of many Pugliese breads.

To make a uniform loaf that can be easily sliced for tramezzini, simply let the rolled dough rise in a loaf pan. For serving as an accompaniment to meals, I like to make a thin long roll and curve it into an undulating serpent shape. We also make sfogliata filled with toasted walnuts and creamy dolcelatte Gorgonzola or with pesto sauce and pine nuts. Let your imagination soar.

1 RECIPE SEMOLINA DOUGH (SEE PAGE 80), ALLOWED TO RISE ONCE
1½ CUPS SUN-DRIED TOMATO PESTO (SEE PAGE 224)
2 PINCHES DRIED OREGANO
1 CUP PITTED KALAMATA OR GAETA OLIVES, COARSELY CHOPPED

Sprinkle a work surface with flour. Punch the dough down and use your fingertips to push it into a rough rectangle. Lightly dust the top of the dough with flour. Roll the dough out to a large ½-inch-thick rectangle. Spread the sun-dried tomato pesto over the dough, leaving a 2-inch border on all sides. Sprinkle the oregano and chopped olives over the pesto. Starting at a long side, roll the dough up into a firm roll. Pinch the seam to keep the filling from oozing out. Pinch the ends and tuck them under. Arrange the roll in the shape you desire on a large oiled baking sheet. Cover the bread with a towel and allow to rise for 1 hour or until nearly doubled in bulk.

Preheat the oven to 350°F.

Bake the bread until light golden brown on the bottom, approximately 30 minutes.

Pane degli Angeli (Angeli Pizza Bread)

Makes 4 loaves

OUR SIGNATURE ANGELI BREAD IS MUCH IN DEMAND and has been imitated all over the city. The ancestor of this homey pizza bread is the Pugliese *puccia*, an individually sized loaf of simple dough shaped into a round and then firmly patted down so that upon baking in a very hot oven what results is a puffy, semihollow pillow loaf. We make ours out of the same dough we use for our pizzas. They are the perfect size for many of the recipes in the panini chapter and can be made smaller if desired for the cicchetti recipes as well.

1 RECIPE PIZZA DOUGH (SEE PAGE 18), SHAPED INTO 4 BALLS AND ALLOWED
TO RISE AS FOR PIZZA MAKING

Place a pizza stone or unglazed tiles on the lowest oven rack. Preheat the oven to 500°F.

Lightly dust each risen dough ball on both sides with flour. Place 1 ball of dough on a floured work surface. Press down on the dough ball firmly with your fingertips until it is flattened to a circle about ½ inch thick; do not stretch out the dough. Repeat with remaining dough balls.

Place 2 flattened dough balls at a time on a floured wooden peel. Shake the wooden peel gently back and forth to make sure the pizza breads are not stuck to it, and quickly slide them onto the hot baking stone. Bake until the bread is puffed up and deep golden brown, about 7 minutes.

Grissini (Breadsticks)

Makes sixty 10-inch breadsticks

WHEN I WAS GROWING UP in the Silverlake area of Los Angeles, Sarno was the Italian bakery in the neighborhood. One of my favorite treats was to go by the bakery on the weekends to see if Signore Gerardo had made any of his extraordinary grissini. They were huge, uneven, and dotted with walnuts—I would make a meal of them. It is easy to vary this recipe to create your own signature grissini. Some flavoring suggestions are walnuts, hazelnuts, Parmesan cheese, and/or poppy, fennel, or sesame seeds. Nuts should be kneaded into the dough before the first rise. Smaller ingredients, such as seeds, need only be sprinkled over the strips before you stretch them out.

You will need a lot of counter space for this recipe, so prepare in advance so you won't be cramped when working. When you stretch out the strips of dough to create the breadsticks, don't worry about making them all the same. Part of their visual charm, as well as their interest in your mouth is the variety of thickness and length. The thinner you stretch them out, the crisper they will be, while the thicker bumps on each stick will be a little chewy. If you have a convection option in your oven, now is the time to use it to create perfectly crispy grissini with a more uniform texture than those baked in a conventional oven.

1 RECIPE PIZZA DOUGH (SEE PAGE 18), PREPARED THROUGH THE FIRST RISE ONLY
EXTRA-VIRGIN OLIVE OIL FOR BRUSHING

On a clean countertop, stretch and press the dough into a rough 12 by 15-inch rectangle, without crushing too much air out of it. Brush olive oil generously over the top of the dough and leave it to rise in a warm place for 1 hour, or until doubled in bulk.

Preheat the oven to 450°F. Rub two baking sheets generously with olive oil.

With a pizza cutter or sharp knife cut the dough in plum-sized pieces and holding them low over a baking sheet, stretch the dough into 10-inch strips, and place on the sheet. Handle the strips carefully to avoid crushing the air out of them.

Bake until crisp and golden, 13 to 16 minutes. Transfer to a rack to cool. Serve warm or at room temperature; do not refrigerate.

Ficatelle (Crunchy Pizza Snacks)

Serves 10

WHEN ANGELI MARE WAS ABOUT TO OPEN, I realized that we needed some bar food to accompany the cocktails we would be serving. Since a bowl of dry salty snacks isn't exactly my idea of pleasure, I searched to find a recipe that would introduce a bit of Angeli at first bite, even over a drink. Ficatelle are light crunchy puffs of deep-fried pizza dough flavored with herbs or prosciutto. The dough is stretched exactly as for pizza, but it is then cut into strips or diamonds and thrown into a pot of hot oil. Add the flavorings to the dough by tossing them with a bit of the flour called for in the recipe so they don't stick together and add them to the rest of the flour.

1 RECIPE PIZZA DOUGH (SEE PAGE 18), PREPARED

1 TABLESPOON FINELY CHOPPED ROSEMARY AND/OR 2 THICK SLICES PROSCIUTTO, CUT INTO 1/4-INCH DICE, ADDED AS DIRECTED ABOVE AND ALLOWED TO RISE ONCE

VEGETABLE OIL FOR DEEP-FRYING

Sprinkle a work surface with flour. Divide the dough into quarters, and roll each piece into a tight smooth ball, kneading it to push the air out of it. Place the dough balls on a lightly floured surface, cover them with a clean kitchen towel, and let rest for 1 hour. (Or place them on a floured towel on a cookie sheet, cover with a towel, and refrigerate overnight. The dough will keep in the refrigerator for approximately 2 days or in the freezer for up to 1 month.

Prepare the dough balls as you would for pizza, stretching it out by hand (or roll it out if you prefer): Place 1 ball of dough on a lightly floured work surface or on a floured peel. Sprinkle a little more flour on top of the ball. Using your fingertips, press the dough down evenly into a large flat disk about ½ inch thick. Lift the dough and lay it over the back of the fist of one hand. Place your other fist underneath the dough so your fists are almost touching. Now gently stretch the dough by moving your fists away from each other; each time you perform this stretching move, rotate the dough. Continue stretching and rotating until the round of dough is about ¼ inch thick and measures about 9 inches across. Repeat with the remaining dough balls.

Heat the vegetable oil in a large heavy saucepan or a deep-fat fryer to 375°F. With a pizza cutter, cut across each dough round to make strips ½ inch wide, then cut across the center of the round to cut the strips in half. Fry the strips of dough, in batches, until they are golden. Drain briefly on paper towels before serving.

pasta:
the essence
of angeli

I have come to believe that there is no food more friendly than pasta.

There is something about the playful shapes and comforting consis-

tency of noodles that, quite simply, makes people very happy. At

Angeli, that means that most of the time we have a dining room filled

with lots of contented people. Pasta is our most popular menu item

year in and year out. The acceptance of Italian pasta has become so

tremendous that I doubt if most Americans even think of it as an ethnic

food anymore. We have embraced it; it is ours.

What the Italian kitchen gives to the world of pasta is clear, vivid flavors combined with ingenious simplicity. A palette of relatively few herbs and condiments is paired almost ritualistically with easily available ingredients to achieve that pop of flavor in the mouth that is so satisfying. Coming from a cuisine born out of poverty, most Italian pasta dishes are vegetable-based, with meat often used more as a condiment or flavoring than a main ingredient. What could be more perfect for a society searching for food that is low-fat, high in complex carbohydrates, vegetarian, but satisfying?

Operating a restaurant as a cookbook author offers up the conundrum of a daily audience that has and frequently uses my previous four books. Our customers expect to see their favorite recipes on the menu from time to time. Since the repertoire consists of literally hundreds of pastas, our solution has been to have daily pastas, "The Classics," which are always available, and then a rotating schedule of four pasta specials a day that remain the same for a season, then change. In that way, over the course of a year I am able to offer our customers more than one hundred different pastas. The great thing about this system is that the seasonal pastas become like "blue plate specials," with many customers coming in once or twice a week for their favorite. The down side is that when the menu changes, our guests often act as if they've lost a friend. But we assure them that they will make new ones quickly!

There are more recipes for baked pastas in this book than in any of my previous efforts. A healthy catering business has developed over the years to serve our customers who wish to share the Caffè food in a party atmosphere. We seem to have a wider-than-average sphere of clients, with our business ranging from once-in-a-life-time events such as weddings, anniversaries, and bar/bat mitzvahs to video and commercial shoots. Since Angeli is so well known for its pasta, it is hard for us to say no to requests or to explain that pasta doesn't hold up well in a chafing dish or on a buffet line. So, over the years we have developed quite a few baked dishes that vary from light and elegant to rustic and gutsy. They are all suitable for large gatherings and have the distinct advantage that they are basically prepared in advance and hold up better during a party.

A few words about buying and cooking pasta: Because so many of the sauces we make have strong, sharp flavors, we use far more dried durum wheat pasta than fresh egg pasta. High-quality durum wheat pasta from Italy has the advantage of both a neutral flavor that shows off strong sauces and a satisfying meaty texture when cooked al dente. At Angeli we use only imported Italian pasta. The brands we choose are Rustichella, Martelli, and DeCecco. Rustichella and Martelli are small family-run businesses that produce an old-style artisan pasta. These are character-ized by reliance on two main techniques, extrusion through bronze dies, producing a highly textured pasta that absorbs sauces beautifully, and slow drying, which allows the pasta to maintain an al dente state, once cooked. Look for imported Italian dried pasta that is of superlative quality. I have yet to find an American brand that fulfills all the requirements of a very finely made dry pasta. It must have a rough, porous texture that will absorb sauce. It must be able to be cooked al dente without becom-ing either chalky or soft. In addition to Rustichella and Martelli, Cavalieri and Latini are high-quality artisan-style Italian brands. These are all beginning to find a good distribution throughout the United States; if they are unavailable, DeCecco is a won-derful standby for everyday use.

That said, there are times when nothing but fresh handmade egg pasta will do. For the many filled and baked pasta dishes I offer here, I include a recipe for fresh pasta. I am assuming that most of you will choose to use a pasta machine for rolling; if you are interested in how to roll pasta out by hand, there's a complete description in *Pasta Fresca*, one of my collaborations with Viana La Place (Morrow, 1988).

Many of the classic dos and don'ts I present here have appeared in my other books, but I don't think it's possible to repeat them enough: Never add oil to pasta cooking water. Never rinse pasta that is to be served hot. All you will be doing by using either of these erroneous techniques is to rid the pasta of the outer sheath of starch that allows the sauce to adhere to the noodle, and you will find your sauce slipping off the noodles into an unattractive pool at the bottom of the plate. Always cook pasta in a big pot of salted boiling water so it has room to move; this prevents sticking, as does stirring the pasta during the first couple of minutes of cooking time.

The first five years in the life of Angeli was also the time Viana La Place and I were working on *Cucina Fresca, Pasta Fresca*, and *Cucina Rustica*. As is natural to expect, many Angeli pastas found their way onto those pages. Here I present our Angeli Classics, as well as a taste of each season.

Pasta Fresca all'Uovo

Makes approximately 1¼ pounds, enough for 4 to 6 servings

A BASIC EGG DOUGH TO ADD TO YOUR REPERTOIRE. If you have a local farmers' market with a vendor of freshly laid eggs, be sure to purchase them for making fresh pasta. The yolks will be a deeper yellow-orange than supermarket eggs and will add greater color and richness to the pasta.

2 CUPS UNBLEACHED ALL-PURPOSE FLOUR

3 EXTRA-LARGE EGGS, BEATEN

To make the pasta dough in a food processor

Place the flour in the bowl of a food processor fitted with the steel blade. Lightly beat the eggs. With the machine running, slowly pour the beaten eggs into the flour. Do not add all the eggs at once because, depending on the humidity, you may not need them all. Pulse the machine until the eggs and flour come together in a stiff mixture. Turn the mixture out onto a floured board and firmly knead it together into a stiff dough. Set the dough aside to rest, covered with a kitchen towel, for 15 minutes.

To make the pasta dough by hand

Make a mound of flour on a wooden or marble slab. Using your fingers, hollow a wide hole out of the center of the mound so that the flour looks like the crater of a volcano. Carefully break each egg separately into a cup to make sure it is fresh and good, then transfer it to the crater. Using a dinner fork with long tines, carefully beat the eggs until they are well scrambled. Keep beating the eggs and begin to slowly incorporate flour from the sides of the crater. Take care that the runny egg-and-flour batter in the crater is kept enclosed on all sides by the flour. When the egg mixture is very thick and you can no longer mix in any more flour with the fork, carefully push the remaining flour over the mixture and begin to knead it with your hands. Continue to knead until the dough absorbs as much flour as possible. After 10 minutes or so of kneading, you should have a stiff but elastic dough. (The beauty of this method is that if you have too much flour for the amount of egg, the extra flour will automatically fall away to the side and will not become incorporated into the dough.) Allow the dough to rest, covered with a kitchen towel, for at least 15 minutes.

To roll pasta using a pasta machine

Uncover the dough, carefully cut off a 1-inch-thick slice, and cover the remaining pasta. Flatten the pasta slice with the heel of your hand. If the dough feels a little tacky, lightly coat each side with flour. Open the pasta-machine rollers to their widest point and feed the pasta through the rollers. Repeat 5 to 6 times, each time folding the sheet of pasta over itself in thirds. You will know when the pasta has been kneaded enough by the dramatic change in texture—it will become very smooth and satiny to the touch. Whenever I teach a class, the students tell me they usually stop kneading before it achieves that satiny consistency. Be patient.

When you are ready to roll the pasta to the thickness you desire, remember that as the sheet of pasta gets thinner, it will also get longer. To make the process more manageable, cut the dough sheet into lengths about 12 inches long. Roll each sheet of pasta, passing it through each numbered setting successively until you achieve the thickness you desire. For stuffed pastas, roll the dough as thin as the machine will allow. For fettuccine, use the second-thinnest setting. Then roll out the remaining dough.

If you are making the pasta sheets, *sfoglie*, for stuffed pasta, use them immediately. To use the sfoglie for fettuccine or other noodles, allow the sheets to dry just enough so that they won't stick to themselves during the cutting process. Lay the sheets of dough on a lightly floured bed-sheet or a few tea towels. Let the pasta dry, turning it occasionally, until it is just dry enough to take on a leathery appearance, yet not so much that it becomes brittle. Drying will take approximately 15 to 30 minutes, depending on how warm and/or humid it is.

angeli classics

The Angeli Classics, or as we say on the menu, Everyday Pasta, are the six pastas that form the backbone of nearly every trattoria menu in Italy. We also offer a vegetarian lasagna for those who are trying to eat less meat. These dishes are designed for those who find satisfaction in simple, familiar dishes made of easily identifiable ingredients. Having said that, for me, they are simply the best . . . a purist's dream. When hunger assaults you and you don't have the energy to face an unknown quantity on your plate, nothing quells the pangs as comfortingly as these dishes.

Spaghetti Aglio e Olio

OIL AND GARLIC

Serves 4 to 6

A SAUCE THAT TRANSCENDS ANY REGIONAL CHAUVINISM. When the palate is jaded and needs simple, strong flavors, no pasta dish is as satisfying as a perfectly made dish of Spaghetti Aglio e Olio. Use real spaghetti for this dish, not spaghettini. Although I've noticed that many of our customers prefer thinner cuts of pasta, the thick, round al dente bite of a spaghetti or even the larger spaghettoni is often better suited to sauces that showcase a few strongly flavored ingredients. Make sure your garlic is young, firm, and unsprouted. Whether you mince, slice, or press the cloves, or keep them whole, is up to you. Each method adds its own characteristic degree of pungency to the dish. Use the best extra-virgin olive oil you have in the house. During summer months, use a fresh hot Italian peperoncino (fresh cayenne pepper) if you can find it; if not, substitute Thai chiles or even red jalapeños. Use dried whole chilies or chile flakes in winter.

> 1/2 TO 3/4 CUP EXTRA-VIRGIN OLIVE OIL (TO TASTE)
>
> 8 GARLIC CLOVES (OR MORE TO TASTE), PEELED AND SLICED
>
> 1/2 FRESH CAYENNE PEPPER OR RED CHILE PEPPER FLAKES TO TASTE
>
> KOSHER SALT TO TASTE
>
> 1/2 LEMON, OR TO TASTE
>
> SMALL HANDFUL OF COARSELY CHOPPED FRESH ITALIAN PARSLEY
>
> 1 POUND IMPORTED ITALIAN SPAGHETTI

Combine the oil, garlic, and hot pepper in a small skillet and cook over low heat until the garlic is barely brown on the edges, or the color you like. Remember that the garlic will keep on cooking even after the heat is turned off, so be careful not to overcook. Remove the pan from the heat, sprinkle in salt to taste and squeeze a bit of lemon juice into the pan. Add the parsley and stir to mix.

Meanwhile, cook the pasta in abundant boiling salted water until al dente. Drain, leaving a bit of moisture clinging to the pasta.

Place the pasta in a serving bowl, add the garlic-oil mixture, and toss well to mix. Serve immediately.

Fettuccine al Burro e Parmigiana

BUTTER AND PARMESAN

Serves 4 to 6

THE ORIGINAL FETTUCCINE ALFREDO, a dish in which the alchemy of the kitchen gods is working overtime as full-fat butter, Parmigiano-Reggiano, and a bit of pasta water are turned into the most comforting of all sauces. If you can find it, buy Plugra to make this dish; Plugra is a high-butterfat pastry butter similar to the butter found on many European tables, and beautifully suited to this dish. Don't be afraid to use dried egg pasta here. A good-quality imported egg fettuccine or pappardelle is usually much tastier than a poorly made batch of industrial fresh pasta. Always be sure not to overcook egg pasta. Even dried, it takes very little time to cook.

> 1 recipe Pasta Fresca all'Uovo (See page 104), cut into fettuccine, or 1 pound imported Italian dried fettuccine or pappardelle
>
> 1 stick (8 tablespoons) unsalted butter, softened
>
> 1 cup grated Italian Parmesan cheese, plus additional for the table
>
> Freshly ground black pepper to taste

Cook the pasta in abundant boiling salted water until al dente. Meanwhile, break the butter up into three or four chunks and place in a serving dish.

Just before you are ready to drain the pasta, ladle out about ¼ cup of the pasta cooking water and reserve it. Drain the pasta, leaving some of the moisture clinging to it. Gently lay the drained pasta over the butter in the serving bowl. Add the Parmesan cheese and pepper and toss the pasta to coat every strand with the butter and Parmesan cheese. Add just enough pasta cooking water to create a creamy sauce. Serve immediately, with additional Parmesan cheese at the table.

Spaghetti alla Marinara

GARLIC, TOMATO SAUCE, OREGANO

Serves 4 to 6

IT IS POSSIBLE TO SEE the word *marinara* on five different Italian menus and have it mean five different sauces that range from a simple tomato sauce with herbs to one of mixed seafood and tomatoes. Piccinardi's *Dizionaria di Gastronomia* defines *alla marinara* as "a generic term that indicates the presence of tomatoes and Mediterranean aromatic herbs such as basil, oregano, olives, capers, etc." At Angeli, we take the reductionist view; our marinara is a simple sauce of tomatoes, oil, garlic, and oregano. Because we want our recipes to be consistent from day to day, we use canned tomatoes in this sauce. That way I know we can prepare the exact same sauce all year round, even when good fresh sauce tomatoes are impossible to find. Most good Italian home cooks would use a bottled *passato di pomodoro*, tomato sauce, that they put up in summer to last through the winter months.

1/4 CUP EXTRA-VIRGIN OLIVE OIL

2 GARLIC CLOVES, PEELED AND SLICED

ONE 28-OUNCE CAN ITALIAN OR ITALIAN-STYLE PEAR TOMATOES WITH JUICE

1/2 TEASPOON DRIED OREGANO

KOSHER SALT AND FRESHLY GROUND BLACK PEPPER TO TASTE

1 POUND IMPORTED ITALIAN SPAGHETTI

GRATED ITALIAN PARMESAN CHEESE FOR THE TABLE (OPTIONAL)

Heat the oil in a large heavy skillet. Add the garlic and cook over medium heat until it gives off its aroma. Lift the tomatoes out of their juice and crush between your fingers while adding them to the skillet along with their juice. Add the oregano, bruising it a bit with your fingers. Stirring frequently, cook until the tomatoes thicken into a sauce, 15 to 20 minutes. Add salt and pepper to taste.

Meanwhile, cook the pasta in abundant boiling salted water until al dente. Quickly drain the pasta and add it to the skillet. Toss the pasta with the hot sauce until it has absorbed a bit of sauce. Serve immediately. Pass Parmesan cheese if desired.

Penne all'Arrabiata

TOMATOES, OIL, HOT PEPPER, GARLIC

Serves 4 to 6

IT'S HARD TO BELIEVE THAT after more than twenty years of intensive food exploration in Italy, I could still be staggered by the superlative quality of the basic ingredients available there. One night in Umbria I experienced one example of what can occur out of the perfection of simplicity. I had just finished a week-long private cooking adventure with four fascinating couples, all of us "chaperoned" by my mother. When they left to pursue other adventures, Mom and I were able to treat ourselves to one final night alone in the restored farmhouse before we decamped to Rome. It was dusk, and as I looked out through the small square windows cut into the stone walls onto the surrounding countryside, I could feel a calming silence enter the house. The walls of the house were tinted purple by the dying sun, and deep shadows started to creep into the crevices of the surrounding gentle hills and meadows. We could hear only an occasional bird cry.

Spent, I wanted to expend as little effort as possible to make our meal. I began by pouring some of my friend Marina Colonna's golden oil into a skillet. A fresh cayenne pepper from a strand hanging over the work area found its way into the pan. I sorted through a bowl of fresh San Marzano tomatoes to find those that were perfectly ripe and broke them up with my fingers, letting the pieces fall onto the coarse blade of my shining-new food mill. The pepper was sizzling in the oil as I added the fresh tomato *passato* to the pan. I reached for the garlic press to press a couple of cloves directly into the sauce. As we listened to the sauce simmer, I put on a pot of water for pasta. When it boiled, I dropped in a couple of nests of *ciriole*, the traditional Umbrian pasta; made from only durum wheat and water, it is like a very thick square spaghetti.

The sauce was scarlet, the pasta off-white. As we took the first fork-twirl from our full bowls, we were blown away. My mother kept repeating "What did you do?" "What did you do?" like a mantra. It's easy to create perfection when you start with it. The single most popular "everyday" sauce at Angeli.

One 28-ounce can Italian or Italian-style pear tomatoes with juice or
12 ripe Roma tomatoes or 6 large ripe round tomatoes, stem ends removed and cut
into quarters

1/4 cup extra-virgin olive oil

1/2 fresh cayenne pepper or red chile pepper flakes to taste

2 to 3 garlic cloves (or to taste), peeled

Kosher salt to taste

1 pound imported Italian penne

Set a food mill over a bowl and puree the tomatoes, using the coarse disk.

Heat the oil in a large heavy skillet over moderate heat. Add the hot pepper. As soon as the oil takes on a bit of color from the chile, add the pureed tomatoes to the skillet and stir them into the oil, mixing well. Squeeze the garlic cloves through a press directly into the sauce. Add salt to taste. Cook over medium heat until the sauce thickens, approximately 15 minutes. The sauce will turn a deep red-orange and flecks of oil will be dispersed through the sauce.

Meanwhile, cook the pasta in abundant boiling salted water until al dente. Quickly drain the pasta and place it in the skillet. Toss the pasta with the hot sauce until it has absorbed a bit of sauce. Serve immediately.

Spaghetti alla Checca

TOMATOES, GARLIC, BASIL, OIL, FRESH MOZZARELLA

Serves 4 to 6

A MODERN TRADITION FROM ROME, this sauce is so popular it's hard to convince people that it's really at its best in summer, when thin-skinned tomatoes heavy with juice are in the market. A simple healthful dish, whose fat content you can control by adding olive oil to taste, it remains on our menu every day, even during winter.

I suggest preparing the tomatoes, oil, and herbs early in the day, perhaps before you leave for work. Set them aside to marinate in a shady part of the kitchen and let sit for a few hours or so. Upon your return, you will find that the natural juice of the tomatoes has mixed with the oil and herbs and the mixture is quite saucy and full of flavor. Then you need simply add the mozzarella and toss the room-temperature sauce with steaming-hot pasta right from the colander so that the tender mozzarella partially melts onto the strands of pasta.

This recipe is a perfect starting point for many room-temperature pastas. Simply add additional ingredients of your choice, such as pitted olives, capers, hot pepper, chopped raw vegetables, or even grilled tuna. We usually use orecchiete instead of spaghetti when serving the pasta to large groups. Its little thumbprint catches the chopped tomatoes and makes the dish easy to serve.

6 RIPE ROMA TOMATOES OR 4 LARGE RIPE ROUND TOMATOES, STEM ENDS REMOVED AND CUT INTO SMALL DICE

1 TO 2 GARLIC CLOVES, PEELED AND MINCED

10 LEAVES FRESH BASIL, COARSELY CHOPPED

KOSHER SALT AND FRESHLY GROUND BLACK PEPPER TO TASTE

EXTRA-VIRGIN OLIVE OIL TO TASTE

6 TO 8 OUNCES FRESH MOZZARELLA CHEESE, DRAINED AND CUT INTO SMALL DICE

1 POUND IMPORTED ITALIAN SPAGHETTI

In a medium bowl, combine the tomatoes, garlic, basil, and salt and pepper to taste. Add as much olive oil as you desire, remembering that the more you add, the more saucy and flavorful the resulting dish will be. Marinate at room temperature for at least 1 hour.

Just before serving, place the tomato mixture in a large serving bowl, add the mozzarella, and mix well.

Meanwhile, cook the pasta in abundant boiling salted water until al dente. Quickly drain the pasta and add it to the serving bowl. Toss the hot pasta with the sauce and serve immediately.

Fettuccine Bolognese

DRIED PORCINI, GROUND BEEF, WINE, HERBS, BROTH

Serves 4 to 6

MANY PEOPLE CONFUSE BOLOGNESE SAUCES with tomato-based ragùs. Bolognese is a meat sauce that has a bit of tomato sauce in it as a flavor enrichment and for color. It is *not* a tomato sauce with meat. Instead of tomato sauce, broth or water is used as a cooking medium for the ground meats. As the liquid reduces, the flavors concentrate to result in an intensely flavored meat broth. The dish is traditionally finished with a bit of unsalted butter and a small handful of grated Parmesan cheese to add a bit of creaminess to the sauce. Here is a classic version of Bolognese that we serve at Angeli. It is a variation of a recipe from Marcella Hazan's *Italian Kitchen,* my first purchase of an Italian cookbook.

1 OUNCE DRIED PORCINI MUSHROOMS

2 TABLESPOONS OLIVE OIL

2 TABLESPOONS UNSALTED BUTTER

1 CELERY STALK, MINCED

1 CARROT, PEELED AND MINCED

1 ONION, PEELED AND MINCED

1 GARLIC CLOVE, PEELED AND MINCED

1 POUND GROUND BEEF CHUCK

1/4 POUND BULK SWEET ITALIAN SAUSAGE

1 CUP RED WINE

SMALL HANDFUL OF COARSELY CHOPPED FRESH ITALIAN PARSLEY

2 TO 3 FRESH SAGE LEAVES OR 1/2 TEASPOON DRIED SAGE

1 BAY LEAF

ONE 14-OUNCE CAN TOMATO PUREE

1 1/2 CUPS CHICKEN OR BEEF BROTH PLUS 1 1/2 CUPS WATER, OR 3 CUPS WATER

KOSHER SALT AND FRESHLY GROUND BLACK PEPPER TO TASTE

1 POUND IMPORTED ITALIAN DRIED FETTUCCINE OR 1 RECIPE PASTA FRESCA ALL'UOVO

(SEE PAGE 104), CUT INTO FETTUCCINE

2 TABLESPOONS UNSALTED BUTTER, SOFTENED

GRATED ITALIAN PARMESAN CHEESE

Cover the porcini mushrooms with warm water in a small bowl. Set aside and let soak while you prepare the other ingredients.

Heat the oil and butter in a large high-sided saucepan over moderate heat. Add the celery, carrot, and onion and sauté until the vegetables are limp and the onion is translucent. Add the garlic and sauté until it releases its fragrance. Add the ground meat and sausage and cook, stirring often to break up the meat, until no trace of pink remains.

Turn the heat to high, add the wine, and let it simmer until the alcohol evaporates, 1 to 2 minutes. Add the parsley, sage, bay leaf, and tomato puree and stir to mix well. Add the broth and/or water and bring to a gentle simmer.

Meanwhile, lift the porcini out of their soaking liquid. Drain the soaking liquid through a coffee filter to remove any dirt. Add the filtered liquid to the sauce.

Check the porcini to be sure they are free of sand and grit, rinsing only if necessary. Coarsely chop them and add to the sauce. Add salt and pepper to taste. Let cook over gentle heat for about 2 hours, stirring frequently. The liquid will reduce, leaving you with a deeply flavored sauce; if the liquid reduces to the point that the sauce is dry, add a bit more water.

Meanwhile, cook the pasta in abundant boiling salted water until al dente. Quickly drain the pasta and place it in a serving bowl with the butter. Add the hot meat sauce and a handful of grated Parmesan. Toss the pasta with the sauce and serve immediately.

Lasagna Angeli

RICOTTA, SPINACH, CARAMELIZED ONIONS, TOMATO-BASIL SAUCE, BÉCHAMEL

Serves 6 to 8

THE FOLK OF SOUTHERN CALIFORNIA have a reputation for being concerned about health and the shape of their bodies. Sometimes I look out into the dining room and see so many perfect bodies and beautiful faces I feel as if I've recently arrived from another planet. Early on, I realized that to keep my customers happy day to day I needed to have a menu filled with vegetarian possibilities. This simple dish, although brimming with creamy goodness, is one of our most popular, especially with those looking to take out a casual dinner for friends and family.

4 TABLESPOONS UNSALTED BUTTER

3 TABLESPOONS ALL-PURPOSE FLOUR

2 CUPS MILK

COARSE SALT AND FRESHLY GROUND BLACK PEPPER TO TASTE

8 OUNCES RICOTTA CHEESE

2 BUNCHES SPINACH, STEMS TRIMMED AND WELL WASHED

2 ONIONS, PEELED, CUT IN HALF LENGTHWISE, AND THINLY SLICED

1/4 CUP EXTRA-VIRGIN OLIVE OIL

1 RECIPE PASTA FRESCA ALL'UOVO (SEE PAGE 104), ROLLED OUT, OR 1 1/2 POUNDS FRESH PASTA SHEETS

1 RECIPE TOMATO-BASIL SAUCE (SEE PAGE 221)

2 CUPS GRATED ITALIAN PARMESAN CHEESE

To make the béchamel, melt the butter in a small saucepan over low heat. Add the flour and stir to form a smooth paste. Meanwhile, heat the milk in a separate saucepan. When it is hot but not boiling, pour it into the roux (butter-flour mixture), stirring constantly with a whisk or a wooden spoon. Cook over low heat, stirring, until the sauce thickens and the floury taste is gone. Season with salt and pepper. Pour into a mixing bowl and set aside to cool.

When the béchamel has cooled to room temperature, add the ricotta and mix well with a whisk or wooden spoon. Set aside.

Put the spinach in a saucepan with just the water that clings to the leaves and sprinkle with a bit of salt. Cover and cook over low heat just until it wilts. Drain. When it is cool enough to handle, squeeze dry and coarsely chop. Set aside.

Cook the onions in the olive oil until very soft and sweet. Season with salt and pepper to taste. Set aside in a small bowl.

Preheat the oven to 375°F. Cook the pasta in abundant boiling salted water just until al dente; drain well.

Ladle just enough of the tomato-basil sauce into a 9 by 13-inch baking dish to thinly coat the bottom. Cover the sauce with a layer of lasagna noodles. Spoon a ladleful of the béchamel-ricotta mixture onto the pasta. Using a rubber spatula, spread it evenly. Spoon a ladleful of the tomato sauce over the béchamel (it does not need to be a perfectly even layer). Sprinkle a bit of the grated Parmesan cheese over the tomato sauce. Make another layer of pasta, and again layer the tomato sauce, béchamel-ricotta mixture, and Parmesan cheese. Evenly distribute the spinach and cooked onions over the top. Cover the vegetables with another layer of pasta and the tomato sauce, the béchamel-ricotta mixture, and Parmesan cheese. Repeat to make one final layer, finishing with a liberal dusting of Parmesan cheese.

Cover with aluminum foil and bake for approximately 30 minutes, or until the lasagna is bubbling hot. Remove the foil for the last 10 minutes of cooking. Let sit for 10 minutes before serving.

springtime

Spring is the longest season in Los Angeles. Temperate days and nights that have a hint of chill typify our weather so we are able to wallow in the best of springtime produce from local gardens and small farms. Greens of every kind, peas with edible pods, or sweet tiny grains tucked into their pods, asparagus, artichokes, leeks, and spring onions are available in an avalanche of variety. All find their way tossed into pasta dishes of every kind. Here is a small glimpse at some of our favorites.

Asparagi alla Salsa Verde

ASPARAGUS, PARSLEY, CAPERS

Serves 4 to 6

ON A RECENT TRIP TO APULIA, the heel of the boot, I found myself browsing at a farmers' market in Gioia del Colle. The stalls were heaped with gorgeous spring produce, but I found the most delicate treat of the day in the arms of a weatherbeaten gypsy. I was ready to breeze past her when she gently touched my elbow. I stopped and looked into her battered wooden box and saw exquisite bundles of wild asparagus. This dish is my homage to her. Make sure the asparagus is as thin as you can find, the tips and stems still tight and firm.

2 BUNCHES THIN FIRM ASPARAGUS, WOODY ENDS TRIMMED

1 PUNCH ARUGULA, STEMS TRIMMED AND WELL WASHED

2 LARGE HANDFULS COARSELY CHOPPED FRESH ITALIAN PARSLEY

1 TABLESPOON CAPERS

10 KALAMATA OR MOROCCAN OIL-CURED OLIVES, PITTED AND COARSELY CHOPPED

4 GREEN ONIONS, TRIMMED AND THINLY SLICED

2 ANCHOVY FILLETS, RINSED AND MINCED

$1/4$ CUP FRESH LEMON JUICE, OR TO TASTE

$1/2$ TO 1 CUP EXTRA-VIRGIN OLIVE OIL (TO TASTE)

RED CHILE PEPPER FLAKES TO TASTE

1 POUND IMPORTED ITALIAN PENNE

GRATED ITALIAN PARMESAN CHEESE FOR THE TABLE

Blanch the asparagus in boiling salted water for 10 seconds. Drain and immediately plunge into a bowl of ice water to stop the cooking and set the color.

When the asparagus is cold to the touch, drain again. Cut the tips off on the diagonal. Continue cutting the stalks on the diagonal to a size that matches the tips. Place in a large serving bowl.

Tear the arugula into bite-sized pieces and place in the bowl with the asparagus. Add the parsley, capers, olives, green onions, and anchovies. Season with the lemon juice, olive oil, and chile pepper flakes. Toss gently to mix and set aside. Cook the pasta in abundant boiling salted water until al dente. Drain and add to asparagus mixture. Toss well. Pass Parmesan cheese at the table.

Farfalle con Gamberi alla Primavera

SHRIMP, ASPARAGUS, CREAM, PEAS, BASIL

Serves 4 to 6

THE TRADITIONAL SPRINGTIME VEGETABLES ASPARAGUS AND PEAS combine with the sweetness of shrimp to create a very pretty dish. On our menu we often give diners the option of a cream addition to our noncream vegetable pastas. For a less rich dish, substitute one cup of the pasta cooking water for the cream to help the sauce "marry" the pasta.

4 TABLESPOONS UNSALTED BUTTER

1 POUND MEDIUM SHRIMP, PEELED AND DEVEINED

1 GARLIC CLOVE, PEELED AND MINCED

1 BUNCH THIN ASPARAGUS

2 CUPS HEAVY CREAM OR HALF-AND-HALF

1 POUND FRESH PEAS, SHELLED, OR ONE 10-OUNCE PACKAGE FROZEN BABY PEAS

1 BUNCH FRESH BASIL, LEAVES ONLY, HALF CHOPPED, HALF LEFT WHOLE

KOSHER SALT AND FRESHLY GROUND BLACK PEPPER TO TASTE

1 POUND IMPORTED ITALIAN FARFALLE

SMALL HANDFUL OF GRATED ITALIAN PARMESAN CHEESE (OPTIONAL), PLUS MORE FOR THE TABLE

Melt the butter in a large skillet and sauté the shrimp and garlic until the shrimp turn pink. Add the asparagus and continue cooking for another minute or so. Add the cream and bring to a gentle simmer. Add the peas, basil, and salt and pepper to taste. Simmer the sauce until the vegetables are just tender and the cream is slightly thickened.

Meanwhile, cook the pasta in abundant boiling salted water until al dente.

Quickly drain the pasta and place it in the pan with the sauce. Add the handful of Parmesan cheese if desired. Gently toss the pasta with the sauce over low heat until the pasta has absorbed a bit of the sauce. Place the pasta in a serving bowl. Dust with grated Parmesan cheese and serve.

Gnocchetti di Barbabietole

BEETS, RICOTTA, PARMESAN, GARLIC

Serves 4

IN THE RESTAURANT BUSINESS, one is often challenged to try to fit traditional foods into modern celebrations. I developed this dish as a way to serve a beautiful plate of purple-flecked magenta dumplings for Valentine's Day. I use a food mill rather than a food processor to puree the beets so that they add texture as well as their amazing color to the dish. The batter for the dumplings will keep perfectly well for at least three days, so you can make the dumpling mixture on the weekend and then spend only a few minutes preparing a very special midweek supper.

3 SMALL OR 1 LARGE BEET, WASHED, TOPS REMOVED AND RESERVED

1 POUND RICOTTA CHEESE

1 LARGE EGG

2 EGG YOLKS

1/2 CUP GRATED ITALIAN PARMESAN CHEESE, PLUS MORE FOR THE TABLE

KOSHER SALT AND FRESHLY GROUND BLACK PEPPER TO TASTE

2/3 CUP UNBLEACHED ALL-PURPOSE FLOUR, PLUS MORE FOR DREDGING

8 TABLESPOONS (1 STICK) UNSALTED BUTTER

2 GARLIC CLOVES, PEELED AND SLICED

Place the beets in a small saucepan and cover with cold water. Bring to a simmer and cook until tender when pierced with a sharp knife. Drain the beets in a colander and run cold water over them until cool enough to touch. Slip the skins off with your hands.

Cut the beets into quarters and pass them through the coarse disk of a food mill into a medium mixing bowl. Add the ricotta, egg, egg yolks, Parmesan cheese, and salt and pepper to taste. Mix well with a whisk or wooden spoon. Add the 2/3 cup flour and whisk together to mix. Set the mixture aside while you cook the greens and bring a large pot of salted water to a gentle simmer.

Wash the reserved beet tops if necessary. Cut the thin stems from the leaves and cut the stems into small dice. Coarsely chop the leaves. Melt the butter in a large skillet with the sliced garlic. When the garlic begins to give off its characteristic aroma, add the chopped beet stems and leaves and salt and pepper to taste. Cover the skillet and cook over low heat until the leaves wilt. Set aside, covered, while you shape and cook the gnocchetti.

Place a bowl of flour for dredging near the stove. Pick up a walnut-sized piece of the beet mixture and drop it into the bowl of flour, carefully turning to coat all sides. Loosely shape it into a short log and gently squeeze it, using the joints of your fingers to create shallow indentations in the dumpling. Slip the dumpling into the pot of gently simmering water, and continue making dumplings. After the dumplings float to the surface of the water, continue to cook for an additional minute or so. Using a slotted spoon, remove them from the water as they are done and place them in the skillet with the beet greens.

When all gnocchetti are in the skillet, gently heat them through over medium heat. Slip the gnocchetti and greens, with the melted butter, into a large serving dish. Top with a liberal dusting of Parmesan cheese and serve.

Cannelloni ai Frutti di Mare

SPINACH, SCALLOPS, SHRIMP, BÉCHAMEL, TOMATO-BASIL SAUCE

Serves 6 to 8

A BEAUTIFULLY ELEGANT DISH OF spinach, scallops, and shrimp wrapped in tender egg pasta and baked with an orangy-red fresh tomato sauce, with a bit of béchamel added for creaminess.

2 SHALLOTS, PEELED AND MINCED

1 GARLIC CLOVE, PEELED AND MINCED

2 TABLESPOONS EXTRA-VIRGIN OLIVE OIL

2 BUNCHES SPINACH, STEMS TRIMMED AND WELL WASHED

KOSHER SALT TO TASTE

1/2 POUND SEA SCALLOPS, COOKED AND CUT IN HALF HORIZONTALLY

1/2 POUND MEDIUM SHRIMP, COOKED, PEELED, AND COARSELY CHOPPED

SMALL HANDFUL OF COARSELY CHOPPED FRESH ITALIAN PARSLEY

JUICE OF 1 LEMON

1 CUP BÉCHAMEL SAUCE (SEE PAGE 222)

FRESHLY GROUND BLACK PEPPER TO TASTE

1 RECIPE PASTA FRESCA ALL'UOVO (SEE PAGE 104), ROLLED OUT AND CUT INTO 10-INCH-LONG SHEETS, OR 3/4 POUND FRESH PASTA SHEETS

1 RECIPE TOMATO-BASIL SAUCE (SEE PAGE 221)

GRATED ITALIAN PARMESAN CHEESE FOR DUSTING

In a medium skillet, cook the shallots and garlic in the olive oil until the shallots wilt and the garlic gives off its characteristic aroma. Add the spinach and a bit of salt. Cover and cook over low heat until the spinach has wilted and is tender. Remove from the heat. Using a slotted spoon, lift the spinach out of the pan, pressing against the sides of the pan to extract as much liquid as possible. Coarsely chop the spinach and place in a large mixing bowl.

Add the scallops, shrimp, parsley, lemon juice, and béchamel to the spinach. Season with salt and pepper and stir well to mix.

To prepare the cannelloni wrappers, cut the sheets of pasta into 5-inch squares. Cook the pasta squares in abundant boiling salted water until al dente. Quickly drain and either place in a bowl filled with ice water or run cold water gently over the pasta to stop the cooking process. Drain the pasta squares well and lay them on kitchen towels.

Preheat the oven to 375°F. Spread a thin layer of tomato-basil sauce over the bottom of a lightly oiled large baking dish.

Arrange 3 tablespoons of the filling evenly along one edge of each cooked pasta square. Carefully roll up the pasta. As you finish each roll, place it seam side down in the baking dish. Top the finished cannelloni with the remaining tomato-basil sauce. Dust lightly with Parmesan cheese. Cover with aluminum foil and bake for 30 minutes, or until the sauce is bubbling and the cannelloni are heated all the way through.

Remove the foil, dust again with Parmesan cheese, and heat until the Parmesan is dotted golden brown.

summertime

Summer in Southern California—hot and dry but usually not too hot or too dry—
allows the sweetness of tomatoes, eggplants, peppers, summer squashes, and herbs
to crowd the farmers' markets. It is a time of year when ingredients seem to combine
themselves with little effort on the part of the cook, and every dish pleases with the
sheer beauty of the colors nature offers to us.

Pomodoro Crudo e Scalogno

TOMATOES, SHALLOTS, GARLIC, BASIL, OIL

Serves 4 to 6

DURING THE SUMMERTIME, we always offer a large assortment of uncooked tomato sauces. Why cook an ingredient that attains perfection at this time of year? We find this sauce to be a perfect base for more complex dishes. Simply add seafood such as shrimp, scallops, or mussels for a delicious room-temperature pasta. If you enjoy the taste of balsamic vinegar, add a drizzle; it will enhance the natural sweetness of the tomatoes.

6 RIPE ROMA TOMATOES OR 4 LARGE RIPE ROUND TOMATOES, STEM ENDS REMOVED AND CUT INTO SMALL DICE

2 SHALLOTS, PEELED AND MINCED

1 GARLIC CLOVE, PEELED AND MINCED

15 LEAVES FRESH BASIL, COARSELY CHOPPED

KOSHER SALT AND FRESHLY GROUND BLACK PEPPER TO TASTE

EXTRA-VIRGIN OLIVE OIL TO TASTE

1 POUND IMPORTED ITALIAN SPAGHETTI

In a medium bowl, combine the tomatoes, shallots, garlic, basil, and salt and pepper to taste. Add as much olive oil as you desire, remembering that the more you add, the more saucy and flavorful the dish will be. Let marinate at room temperature for at least 1 hour.

Cook the pasta in abundant boiling salted water until al dente. Quickly drain the pasta and place it in a serving bowl. Toss the hot pasta with the sauce and serve immediately.

Linguine ai Fiori di Zucca

ZUCCHINI FLOWERS, BASIL

Serves 4 to 6

THIS RECIPE IS A PERFECT EXAMPLE of the kind of dish that can grow out of cruising the local farmers' market. I know that summertime is here when I see batches of bright yellow squash flowers bundled together, their firm blossoms open wide, ready for the kitchen. Often the small flowers found at the end of baby zucchini are not the best for cooking. Male blossoms are not attached to fruit, but instead have a slender stem. They are usually larger than female blossoms and remain firm and fresh longer.

10 LARGE SQUASH FLOWERS

1 SMALL ONION, PEELED, CUT IN HALF LENGTHWISE, AND THINLY SLICED

1 BULB FENNEL, TOUGH OUTER LAYERS DISCARDED, CORED, AND FEATHERY TOPS RESERVED FOR GARNISH

1/4 CUP EXTRA-VIRGIN OLIVE OIL

2 GARLIC CLOVES, PEELED AND THINLY SLICED

3 SMALL FIRM ZUCCHINI, ENDS TRIMMED, CUT IN HALF LENGTHWISE, AND THINLY SLICED

SMALL HANDFUL OF COARSELY CHOPPED FRESH ITALIAN PARSLEY

10 FRESH WHOLE BASIL LEAVES

KOSHER SALT AND FRESHLY GROUND BLACK PEPPER TO TASTE

1 POUND IMPORTED ITALIAN LINGUINE

HANDFUL OF GRATED ITALIAN PARMESAN CHEESE

Gently wipe any dirt off the squash flowers with a damp towel. With your fingers, reach into the blossoms and pinch out the pistils; discard. Tear the flowers in half lengthwise. Set aside.

Cook the onion and fennel in the oil over medium heat until tender. Add the garlic, zucchini, squash flowers, parsley, basil, and salt and pepper. Cook over high heat, stirring frequently just until the zucchini is tender.

Meanwhile, cook the pasta in abundant boiling salted water until al dente. Just before the pasta is ready to be drained, add 1 cup of the pasta cooking water to the vegetable mixture.

Drain the pasta and place in a serving bowl. Add the Parmesan cheese and the vegetable mixture. Mix well and serve immediately.

Linguine Aglio e Olio alla Siciliana

GARLIC, RED CHILE PEPPER, CAPERS, ANCHOVY, OLIVES, MINT, WILD FENNEL, BREAD CRUMBS
Serves 4 to 6

THE ADDITION OF FENNEL TOPS, MINT, and the traditional Sicilian *sfincioni* ingredients, bread crumbs, olives, capers, and anchovy, enriches a simple dish of pasta aglio e olio. In Southern California, we are lucky to find hillsides and empty lots generously dotted with wild fennel plants. Unlike the domestic variety, wild fennel has no bulb, just masses of fragrant, licorice-scented foliage. If wild fennel doesn't grow in your neighborhood, substitute regular fennel tops. When we need it, my intrepid chef, Kathy Ternay, simply pulls her car off the road at the first glimpse of the feathery green tops, clambers up the hill away from traffic, and hacks down the youngest and most lush and tender wild fennel. She arrives at the Caffè with a grin on her face, arms full of the sweet-smelling plants.

1/2 TO 3/4 CUP EXTRA-VIRGIN OLIVE OIL

8 GARLIC CLOVES (OR MORE TO TASTE), PEELED AND SLICED

1/2 FRESH CAYENNE PEPPER OR RED CHILE PEPPER FLAKES TO TASTE

2 TEASPOONS CAPERS

1 ANCHOVY FILLET PACKED IN SALT OR 2 ANCHOVY FILLETS PACKED IN OIL, RINSED AND CHOPPED

10 KALAMATA OLIVES, PITTED AND TORN IN HALF (OPTIONAL)

1/4 CUP FINELY CHOPPED FRESH MINT

COARSE SALT TO TASTE

1 POUND IMPORTED ITALIAN LINGUINE FINI

1 RUSSET POTATO, PEELED AND CUT INTO SMALL DICE (OPTIONAL)

1 CUP FINELY CHOPPED WILD FENNEL OR FENNEL TOPS

1 CUP GARLICKY BREAD CRUMBS (SEE PAGE 228)

In a large skillet, combine the oil, garlic, hot pepper, capers, anchovy, and olives and cook over low heat until the garlic is the color you like. (Remember that the garlic will keep on cooking after the pan is removed from the heat, so be careful not to overcook it.) Remove from the heat and add the mint and salt to taste. Stir to mix.

Meanwhile, cook the pasta, potato, and fennel together in abundant boiling salted water until the pasta is al dente. Drain, leaving a bit of moisture clinging to the pasta.

Place the pasta, potato, and fennel in a serving bowl and add the garlic-oil mixture and bread crumbs. Toss well to mix. Serve immediately.

Ravioli di Melanzane al Pomodoro Crudo

EGGPLANT PUREE, UNCOOKED TOMATO SAUCE, PARMESAN

Serves 6 to 8

THERE IS SOMETHING ESPECIALLY COMFORTING ABOUT RAVIOLI. Maybe the pillow shape sublimi-
nally reminds us of a relaxing nap or perhaps it's the surprise inherent in every stuffed pasta. If the
filling is homemade, you're usually in for a treat, a combination of flavors not otherwise experienced
in quite the same way. In this summery dish, delicate egg pasta is filled with a tender stuffing of well-
seasoned roasted eggplant puree and then topped with a fresh uncooked sauce of finely diced tomatoes, basil, pine nuts, and olive oil.

FOR THE FILLING

2 FIRM MEDIUM EGGPLANT

3 GARLIC CLOVES, PEELED AND MINCED

Small handful of coarsely chopped fresh Italian parsley

1½ cups grated Italian Parmesan cheese

½ cup dry bread crumbs

2 large eggs

Kosher salt and freshly ground black pepper to taste

FOR THE SAUCE

6 ripe Roma tomatoes or 3 large ripe round tomatoes, stem ends removed and cut
into small dice

1 garlic clove, peeled and minced

15 leaves fresh basil, coarsely chopped

Kosher salt and freshly ground black pepper to taste

½ to 1 cup extra-virgin olive oil (to taste)

1 recipe Pasta Fresca all'Uovo (see page 104)

1 large egg, beaten, for egg wash

Grated Italian Parmesan cheese for dusting

Toasted pine nuts for garnish

A few fresh basil leaves for garnish

To make the filling, preheat the oven to 375°F. Place the eggplant on a baking sheet and prick in a few places with the tip of a sharp paring knife. Bake until the eggplant collapses on itself and the flesh is completely soft, approximately 40 minutes. Remove from the oven and set aside until cool enough to handle.

Cut the eggplant in half. Using a large kitchen spoon, scrape the flesh out of the eggplant shell and place in a colander to drain. When it is well drained, place the eggplant pulp on a cutting board and coarsely chop. Place the pulp in a mixing bowl. Add the garlic, parsley, Parmesan cheese, bread crumbs, eggs, and salt and pepper to taste. Stir well to mix. Set aside.

To make the sauce, in a medium bowl, combine the tomatoes, garlic, basil, and salt and pepper to taste. Add as much olive oil as you desire, remembering that the more you add, the more saucy and flavorful the sauce will be. Let marinate at room temperature for at least 1 hour.

To make the ravioli, using a pasta machine, roll out the dough through the thinnest setting, cutting it into sheets of manageable length, as necessary. Do not roll out too many sheets at a time, or the dough will begin to dry out and become difficult to handle. Make a lengthwise row of scant tablespoons of filling, 1 inch apart, about 1 inch from the bottom edge of one pasta sheet. Brush the egg wash over all the borders. Carefully fold the sheet in half toward you, matching the horizontal edges of the dough. Gently press the pasta down around the mounds of filling to enclose it.

Using a pasta cutter-crimper, trim the edges of the dough and cut apart the ravioli. Lay the ravioli on a lightly floured bedsheet or tea towels. Let dry at least 5 minutes before cooking.

Cook the ravioli in abundant boiling salted water until al dente; very fresh pasta only takes 2 to 5 minutes to cook. Lift the ravioli out of the boiling water with a slotted spoon or Chinese skimmer. Let the spoon or skimmer rest for a moment on a folded terry-cloth towel to absorb some of the cooking water, then gently lay the ravioli in a serving dish. Top with a light dusting of Parmesan cheese, then spoon on the raw tomato sauce. Garnish with pine nuts and whole basil leaves.

Penne Melanzane

MEAT-ENRICHED TOMATO SAUCE, EGGPLANT, FRESH MOZZARELLA

Serves 4 to 6

THIS IS THE SINGLE MOST POPULAR daily pasta special at Angeli. Every time I try to take it off one of our seasonal menus, there is an uproar. So it stays on, through summer, fall, winter, and spring.

¼ CUP EXTRA-VIRGIN OLIVE OIL

4 GARLIC CLOVES, PEELED

¼ SLAB PORK RIBS (APPROXIMATELY ¾ POUND)

8 RIPE ROUND TOMATOES, PEELED, SEEDED, AND CUT INTO QUARTERS, OR ONE 28-OUNCE CAN ITALIAN OR ITALIAN-STYLE PEAR TOMATOES WITH JUICE

ONE 16-OUNCE CAN TOMATO SAUCE (IF USING CANNED TOMATOES)

10 FRESH BASIL LEAVES, COARSELY CHOPPED

KOSHER SALT AND FRESHLY GROUND BLACK PEPPER TO TASTE

OLIVE OIL FOR DEEP FRYING

1 LARGE EGGPLANT, ENDS TRIMMED, PEELED, AND CUT INTO ½-INCH DICE

1 POUND IMPORTED ITALIAN PENNE

8 OUNCES FRESH MOZZARELLA CHEESE, DRAINED AND CUT INTO SMALL DICE

GRATED ITALIAN PARMESAN CHEESE FOR THE TABLE

Heat the oil with the garlic in a heavy saucepan. Cook the garlic until it is a deep golden brown, then remove the cloves from the pan and discard. Add the pork ribs to the pan and brown them well on all sides. Remove from the heat and set aside.

Puree the tomatoes, with their juice if using canned tomatoes, using the coarse disk of a food mill, or in a food processor fitted with the steel blade. Pour the tomato puree into the pot with the ribs. Add the tomato sauce, if using canned tomatoes, and the basil. Bring to a simmer, stirring frequently. Add salt and pepper to taste and cook over medium-high heat until the sauce thickens, about 30 minutes. Remove the ribs and let anyone who helped cook enjoy them as a special treat.

While the sauce is cooking, pour oil to a depth of 2 inches into a large skillet. Add one cube of eggplant to the skillet and heat over medium-high heat until the cube starts to sizzle. Add half of the diced eggplant and sauté until golden brown. Carefully lift out of the hot oil, using a slotted spoon, and place on paper towels to drain. Cook the rest of the eggplant in the same manner.

Cook the pasta in abundant boiling salted water until al dente. Carefully drain the pasta and place it in a serving bowl. Add the tomato sauce, cooked eggplant and mozzarella and toss well to mix. Serve immediately with Parmesan cheese at the table.

Rotolini al Salmone

SALMON, POTATO, ROASTED RED PEPPERS, BÉCHAMEL

Serves 6 to 8

A DELICATE DISH OF BEAUTIFUL COLORS. The salmon-potato filling is spread over fresh pasta sheets lined with roasted red pepper, then rolled up to form elegant rolls. They are then simply finished with a fresh tomato-basil sauce. The perfect entrée for a special dinner when you want to prepare everything in advance so you can enjoy your guests.

1 ONION, PEELED AND THINLY SLICED

1 POUND SALMON FILLET, SKIN REMOVED

3 RIPE TOMATOES, STEM ENDS REMOVED AND THINLY SLICED

KOSHER SALT AND FRESHLY GROUND BLACK PEPPER TO TASTE

1 RECIPE PASTA FRESCA ALL'UOVO (SEE PAGE 104), ROLLED OUT AND CUT INTO

10-INCH-LONG SHEETS, OR 3/4 POUND FRESH PASTA SHEETS

1 RUSSET POTATO, BOILED, PEELED, AND CHOPPED

4 ROASTED RED PEPPERS (SEE PAGE 227) OR ONE 16-OUNCE JAR ROASTED RED PEPPERS

3 CUPS BÉCHAMEL SAUCE (SEE PAGE 222)

GRATED ITALIAN PARMESAN CHEESE

To prepare the filling, preheat the oven to 400°F. Place the onion in a shallow layer in the bottom of a small oiled or buttered baking dish. Top with the salmon fillet. Arrange the sliced tomatoes atop the salmon. Season to taste with salt and pepper. Bake for 10 minutes per inch of thickness of salmon fillet. Set the salmon aside until cool enough to handle, then coarsely chop the salmon, onion, and tomatoes. Reduce the oven temperature to 350°F.

Meanwhile, to prepare the cannelloni wrappers, cut the sheets of pasta into 5-inch squares. Cook the pasta squares in abundant boiling salted water until al dente. Quickly drain and either place in a bowl filled with ice water or run cold water gently over the cooked pasta to stop the cooking process. Drain the pasta squares well and lay them on kitchen towels while you put together the filling.

In a medium mixing bowl, mix together the salmon-onion mixture and the potato. Adjust the seasoning if necessary.

Lay a piece of roasted red pepper approximately 4 inches square over each square of pasta, shiny side down. Spread 3 tablespoons of filling evenly over each pepper, leaving a 1-inch border along the far edge of each square. Starting from the edge nearest you, carefully roll up the pasta. As you finish the rolls, place them seam side down in a lightly oiled large baking dish.

Drizzle the béchamel over the cannelloni and dust lightly with Parmesan cheese. Bake in the 350°F oven for 30 minutes, or until the sauce is bubbling and the cannelloni are heated all the way through.

Orecchiette alla Griglia

CHICKEN, GRILLED VEGETABLES, HERBS, BALSAMIC VINEGAR
Serves 4 to 6

THE PERFECT DISH TO PREPARE FOR A CROWD. If you wish to serve it at room temperature, simply rinse the al dente pasta in cold water, drain, and toss with the grilled chicken and vegetables. The balsamic vinegar adds its tart-sweet bite as well as its deep color to burnish the dish.

3 BONELESS, SKINLESS CHICKEN BREASTS

1 RED ONION, PEELED AND CUT INTO THICK SLICES

1 BULB FENNEL, TOUGH OUTER LAYERS DISCARDED, CORED, AND SLICED

2 SMALL FIRM ZUCCHINI, ENDS TRIMMED AND CUT LENGTHWISE INTO THIN SLICES

2 YELLOW PATTYPAN SQUASH, TRIMMED AND CUT INTO THIN SLICES

2 RED, YELLOW, OR ORANGE BELL PEPPERS, CUT IN HALF LENGTHWISE AND STEMS, SEEDS, AND TOUGH WHITE RIBS REMOVED

10 MEDIUM ASPARAGUS SPEARS, WOODY ENDS TRIMMED

1 SMALL EGGPLANT, ENDS TRIMMED AND THINLY SLICED

OLIVE OIL FOR BRUSHING

Kosher salt and freshly ground black pepper to taste

3 garlic cloves, peeled and minced

Large handful of coarsely chopped fresh Italian parsley

20 fresh basil leaves, coarsely chopped

Extra-virgin olive oil to taste

$\frac{1}{4}$ to $\frac{1}{2}$ cup balsamic vinegar (to taste)

1 pound imported Italian orecchiette

Grated Italian Parmesan cheese for the table

Heat a gas or charcoal grill or ridged stovetop griddle until medium-hot; if a grill or griddle is unavailable, preheat the broiler. Lightly dip an old cloth or towel in vegetable oil and use it to rub the grill grates clean.

Lightly brush the chicken and vegetables with olive oil. Season with salt and pepper. Grill or broil the chicken for approximately 5 minutes per side, or until the juices run clear. Remove from the grill and place on a plate. Grill the vegetables until well marked from the grill on both sides and al dente—except for the eggplant, which should be grilled until tender. As the vegetables are done, remove them from the grill with tongs and place in a large bowl.

Drain any chicken juices from the plate into the bowl of grilled vegetables. Place the chicken on a cutting board and cut crosswise into thin slices, then cut each slice in half. Set aside. Cut all the vegetables into a rough julienne and return to the large bowl. Add the chicken, garlic, herbs, olive oil, and balsamic vinegar and mix well. Adjust the seasoning if necessary. Set aside in a cool spot in the kitchen to marinate for at least 1 hour.

Cook the pasta in abundant boiling salted water until al dente. Drain the pasta and add to the chicken-vegetable mixture. Toss well and place in a serving bowl. Pass Parmesan cheese at the table.

Spaghetti Bellini nel modo d'Angeli

FENNEL, FRESH TOMATOES, EGGPLANT, RICOTTA SALATA

Serves 4 to 6

ONE OF SICILY'S MOST FAMOUS SAUCES is named for the opera composer Vincenzo Bellini. A magic synergy happens when the tomato sauce combines in your mouth with the crisp pieces of eggplant and the pungent creamy bite of the aged ricotta. At Angeli we are big fans of fresh fennel, so we give this traditional pasta a tweak by adding some to the tomato sauce. It gives additional sweetness and complexity to an already superlative dish. Look for round bulbs of fennel; they tend to be much sweeter than the flat ones.

1/4 CUP EXTRA-VIRGIN OLIVE OIL

2 FENNEL BULBS, TOUGH OUTER LAYERS DISCARDED, CUT IN HALF LENGTHWISE, CORED, AND CUT INTO THIN SLICES

2 GARLIC CLOVES, PEELED AND MINCED

12 ROMA TOMATOES, PEELED, SEEDED, AND COARSELY CHOPPED

10 LARGE FRESH BASIL LEAVES

KOSHER SALT AND FRESHLY GROUND BLACK PEPPER TO TASTE

OLIVE OIL FOR FRYING

3 JAPANESE EGGPLANTS, ENDS TRIMMED AND THINLY SLICED

1 POUND IMPORTED ITALIAN SPAGHETTI

4 OUNCES RICOTTA SALATA CHEESE, GRATED

GRATED ITALIAN PARMESAN CHEESE FOR THE TABLE

Heat the extra-virgin oil in a large skillet over medium heat. Sauté the fennel just until it begins to turn limp. Add the garlic and cook until it gives off its characteristic aroma. Add the tomatoes and cook over medium-high heat, stirring frequently, until they begin to break down and form a sauce. Add the basil, season with salt and pepper, cook, stirring occasionally, until the sauce is thick and no longer watery.

While the sauce is cooking, pour enough olive oil into a large skillet to come ½ inch up the side. When the oil is very hot but not smoking, add a single layer of eggplant slices to the pan, being careful not to crowd them, and cook until crisp and golden. Drain on paper towels and sprinkle lightly with coarse salt. Keep warm in a low oven while you cook the remaining eggplant, adding more oil to the pan as necessary.

Cook the pasta in abundant salted water until al dente. Drain the pasta, place it in the skillet with the tomato sauce, and toss it with the sauce over low heat, allowing it to absorb some of the sauce.

Place the pasta in a serving dish. Completely cover the top of the pasta with the fried eggplant rounds. Finish with a sprinkling of ricotta salata over all. Pass Parmesan cheese at the table.

autumn

Autumn is the season when we begin the round of year-end celebrations with family and friends. The cornucopia of hard-shell squashes, wild and domestic mushrooms, and colorful chicories give a rustic earthiness to our palates.

Pappardelle con Zucca e Funghi

BUTTERNUT SQUASH, THYME, SHIITAKE MUSHROOMS, CREAM, WALNUTS

Serves 4 to 6

THE DEEP GOLDEN-BROWN COLORS OF AUTUMN are presented at table with this pasta. We usually use winter squash to fill ravioli, but the combination of tender butternut squash, shiitake mushrooms, walnuts, and thyme goes beautifully with the substantial delicacy of pappardelle to create a perfect holiday dish.

1/2 LARGE BUTTERNUT SQUASH (HALVED LENGTHWISE)

KOSHER SALT AND FRESHLY GROUND BLACK PEPPER TO TASTE

6 TABLESPOONS UNSALTED BUTTER

GRATED ITALIAN PARMESAN CHEESE

1 SMALL ONION, PEELED AND MINCED

1 SHALLOT, PEELED AND MINCED

1 SPRIG THYME, LEAVES ONLY, OR 1/8 TEASPOON DRIED THYME

8 OUNCES SHIITAKE MUSHROOMS, STEMS REMOVED, WIPED CLEAN, AND THINLY SLICED

2 CUPS HEAVY CREAM OR HALF-AND-HALF

1 POUND IMPORTED ITALIAN DRIED PAPPARDELLE OR 1 1/4 POUNDS FRESH PAPPARDELLE

1/2 CUP COARSELY CHOPPED TOASTED WALNUTS

Preheat the oven to 375°F.

Place the squash on a baking sheet, cut side up. Season with salt and pepper to taste. Place 2 tablespoons of the butter in the cavity and dust lightly with Parmesan cheese. Cover loosely with aluminum foil. Bake for 40 minutes, then remove the foil and bake for an additional 20 minutes, or until tender when pierced with a knife. Remove from the oven and let cool. When the squash is cool enough to handle, remove and discard the skin. Coarsely chop the squash pulp and set aside.

Melt the remaining 4 tablespoons butter in a large skillet. Sauté the onion, shallot, and thyme over medium heat until the onion is limp and translucent. Add the shiitakes, turn the heat up to high, and sauté until the mushrooms are soft and golden. Add the cream and squash and season with salt and pepper to taste. Bring the cream to a gentle simmer, gently tossing the ingredients to mix. Add a small handful of Parmesan cheese to the sauce and continue to cook until the cream reduces slightly.

Meanwhile cook the pasta in abundant boiling salted water until al dente.

Quickly drain the pasta and place it in the pan with the sauce. Add the walnuts and gently toss the pasta with the sauce over low heat just until it has absorbed some of the sauce. Place the pasta in a serving bowl. Dust with grated Parmesan cheese and serve.

Salsa ai Funghi Crudi e Pinoli

RADICCHIO, ARUGULA, MUSHROOMS, CARAMELIZED GARLIC, PINE NUTS, PARSLEY

Serves 4 to 6

DURING THE AUTUMN SEASON, the weather is often still quite fair in Los Angeles, with temperatures in the seventies and eighties a common occurrence. Our challenge is to present dishes that feature seasonal produce but are prepared with a light touch for the palate. This dish, lovely with the deep magenta of radicchio and dark green of arugula, offers the lightness of a salad with the traditional deep flavors of autumn. It is also excellent as a room-temperature pasta. Fusilli lunghi is a wonderful pasta that seems to be easier to find these days. It's a long, wavy shape that holds the sauce ingredients very well in its grasp.

1 HEAD RADICCHIO, CORED AND WASHED

2 BUNCHES ARUGULA, TOUGH STEMS TRIMMED AND WELL WASHED

1 POUND CREMINI MUSHROOMS, TRIMMED, WIPED CLEAN, AND SLICED

1 POUND WHITE MUSHROOMS, TRIMMED, WIPED CLEAN, AND SLICED

1/4 CUP CARAMELIZED GARLIC (SEE PAGE 228), COARSELY CHOPPED

1/4 CUP TOASTED PINE NUTS

LARGE HANDFUL OF COARSELY CHOPPED FRESH ITALIAN PARSLEY

EXTRA-VIRGIN OLIVE OIL TO TASTE

CHAMPAGNE VINEGAR TO TASTE

KOSHER SALT AND FRESHLY GROUND BLACK PEPPER TO TASTE

1 POUND IMPORTED ITALIAN FUSILLI LUNGHI OR ORECCHIETTE

GENEROUS HANDFUL OF GRATED ITALIAN PARMESAN CHEESE, PLUS MORE FOR THE TABLE

Separate the radicchio leaves and tear them lengthwise in half; tear very large leaves in half again. Place in a large salad bowl. Tear the arugula leaves in half and add to the bowl. Add the sliced mushrooms, caramelized garlic, pine nuts, and parsley to the bowl. Toss well to mix. Add olive oil and vinegar to taste, season with salt and pepper, and toss well to mix. Set aside so that the ingredients can "cook" in the marinade.

Cook the pasta in abundant boiling salted water until al dente. Drain well and add to the salad bowl with the Parmesan cheese. Toss well. Pass additional Parmesan cheese at the table.

Lasagna ai Funghi

BÉCHAMEL, RICOTTA, SHIITAKE AND CREMINI MUSHROOMS, HERBS, TOMATO-BASIL SAUCE

Serves 6 to 8

THIS IS THE LASAGNA I SEEM TO BRING HOME for my own gatherings with friends more often than any other. The luscious sauce envelops the woodsy mushrooms to create a velvety texture in the mouth.

4 TABLESPOONS UNSALTED BUTTER

3 TABLESPOONS UNBLEACHED ALL-PURPOSE FLOUR

2 CUPS MILK

KOSHER SALT AND FRESHLY GROUND BLACK PEPPER TO TASTE

8 OUNCES RICOTTA CHEESE

1 GARLIC CLOVE, PEELED AND MINCED

1/4 CUP EXTRA-VIRGIN OLIVE OIL

1/2 POUND SHIITAKE MUSHROOMS, STEMS REMOVED, WIPED CLEAN, AND SLICED

1/2 POUND CREMINI MUSHROOMS, STEMS TRIMMED, WIPED CLEAN, AND SLICED

SMALL HANDFUL OF COARSELY CHOPPED FRESH ITALIAN PARSLEY

1 SPRIG ROSEMARY, LEAVES ONLY, MINCED

1 RECIPE PASTA FRESCA ALL'UOVO (SEE PAGE 104), ROLLED OUT AND CUT INTO

13-INCH-LONG SHEETS, OR 1 POUND FRESH PASTA SHEETS

4 CUPS TOMATO-BASIL SAUCE (SEE PAGE 221)

1 TO 2 CUPS GRATED ITALIAN PARMESAN CHEESE

To make the béchamel, melt the butter in a small saucepan over low heat. Add the flour and stir to form a smooth paste. Meanwhile, heat the milk in a separate saucepan. When it is hot but not boiling, pour it into the roux (butter-flour mixture), stirring constantly with a whisk or a wooden spoon. Cook over low heat, stirring, until the sauce thickens and the floury taste is gone. Season with salt and pepper. Pour into a mixing bowl and set aside to cool.

When the béchamel has cooled to room temperature, add the ricotta and mix well with a whisk or wooden spoon. Set aside.

In a large skillet, sauté the garlic in the olive oil until it begins to give off its characteristic aroma. Add the shiitakes and sauté over medium heat until they begin to soften. Add the cremini, parsley, rosemary, and salt and pepper to taste. Turn up the heat to medium-high and continue to sauté, stirring frequently, until the mushrooms are tender and have given up their moisture. Transfer to a bowl and set aside.

Preheat the oven to 375°F.

Cook the pasta in abundant boiling salted water until al dente; drain well.

Ladle just enough of the tomato-basil sauce into the bottom of a 9 by 13-inch baking dish to thinly coat the bottom. Cover the sauce with a layer of lasagna noodles. Spoon a ladleful of the béchamel-ricotta mixture onto the pasta. Using a rubber spatula, spread it evenly. Spoon a ladleful of the tomato sauce over the béchamel. (It does not need to be a perfectly even layer.) Sprinkle a bit of grated Parmesan cheese over the tomato sauce. Make another layer of pasta, and again layer the tomato sauce, béchamel-ricotta mixture, and Parmesan cheese. Evenly distribute half the mushroom mixture over the top. Cover the mushrooms with another layer of pasta and then of tomato sauce, the béchamel-ricotta mixture, and Parmesan cheese. Distribute the remaining mushrooms over the sauce and top with a layer of pasta. Continue layering the ingredients, finishing with a liberal dusting of Parmesan cheese.

Cover with aluminum foil and bake for approximately 30 minutes, or until the lasagna is bubbling hot. Remove foil for the last 10 minutes of cooking. Let sit for 10 minutes before serving.

Classic All-Purpose Polenta

Makes 6 servings soft polenta or 1 loaf

THE HARD TRUTH ABOUT POLENTA IS that the longer you stir it, the better it is. It is certainly possible to make it with less water, so that it thickens more quickly, but the individual stone-ground grains of corn will still be tough. I prefer to take the time so that the result is a toothsome mound of gold, ready to receive its topping. I stopped purchasing imported Italian polenta after too many negative experiences of finding it to be tasteless. I prefer the sweet freshness of coarse stone-ground corn grits (identical to polenta) found in most natural food stores.

6½ CUPS WATER OR HALF WATER AND HALF CHICKEN BROTH

2 TEASPOONS SALT

6 TABLESPOONS UNSALTED BUTTER

1½ CUPS STONE-GROUND COARSE GRITS OR IMPORTED POLENTA

LARGE HANDFUL OF GRATED ITALIAN PARMESAN CHEESE

Bring the water to a boil and add the salt and 4 tablespoons of the butter. When the water returns to the boil, whisk in the grits, adding it in a slow, steady stream. Reduce the heat to medium and, with the whisk or a wooden spoon, cook, stirring continuously, for approximately 40 minutes, or until the polenta is thick enough to grab the whisk yet is still soft, like a very thick porridge.

Beat in the Parmesan cheese and the remaining 2 tablespoons butter. The polenta is ready to serve.

For baked, grilled, or fried polenta, pour the hot polenta into a loaf pan or baking dish. Smooth the top with a rubber spatula and set it aside to cool. (You can make the polenta up to 3 days in advance and refrigerate it.) Once chilled, the polenta can be sliced and grilled, fried, or used in a baked casserole.

Polenta ai Ragù di Funghi

MUSHROOMS, HERBS, PINE NUTS

Serves 4 to 6

WHEN I AM ASKED TO PARTICIPATE IN SPECIAL EVENTS during the fall and winter months, this is the dish I like to present. As rich and tasty as a meat-based stew, it is the perfect way to introduce soft polenta to a new audience. The stew is redolent with the specific flavor of the different mushrooms, the woodsy rosemary, and the toasted pine nuts.

$1/4$ CUP DRIED PORCINI MUSHROOMS

$1/4$ CUP EXTRA-VIRGIN OLIVE OIL

3 GARLIC CLOVES, PEELED AND MINCED

$1/2$ POUND SHIITAKE MUSHROOMS, STEMS REMOVED, WIPED CLEAN, AND SLICED

1 POUND CREMINI OR WHITE MUSHROOMS, TRIMMED, WIPED CLEAN, AND SLICED

4 RIPE TOMATOES, DICED

GENEROUS HANDFUL OF CHOPPED FRESH ITALIAN PARSLEY AND FRESH BASIL

PINCH OF FINELY CHOPPED FRESH ROSEMARY

4 CUPS WATER OR CHICKEN BROTH

1 CUP TOMATO-BASIL SAUCE (SEE PAGE 221) OR PREPARED TOMATO SAUCE

$1/4$ CUP LIGHTLY TOASTED PINE NUTS

KOSHER SALT AND FRESHLY GROUND BLACK PEPPER TO TASTE

1 RECIPE CLASSIC ALL-PURPOSE POLENTA (SEE PAGE 149)

GRATED ITALIAN PARMESAN CHEESE FOR DUSTING

Cover the porcini mushrooms with 1 cup hot water and let stand 20 minutes. Remove the porcini, reserving the soaking liquid, and coarsely chop them. Strain the liquid through a paper coffee filter or cheesecloth.

Heat the olive oil in a large heavy-bottomed skillet. Sauté the garlic in the oil until it releases its characteristic aroma. Add the porcini, shiitake, and cremini mushrooms and sauté until the mushrooms begin to release their liquid. Add the diced tomatoes and herbs and cook until the tomatoes begin to get saucy. Add the water or chicken broth, tomato-basil sauce, the reserved porcini soaking liquid, and the pine nuts and simmer until the sauce is reduced slightly but not too thick. Season with salt and pepper to taste. Set the mushroom ragù aside while you prepare the polenta.

When the polenta is thick and ready to serve spoon it into individual pasta bowls or onto a serving platter, and create a shallow crater in the center with the back of the spoon. Ladle the mushroom ragù into the indentation. Dust with Parmesan cheese and serve immediately.

wintertime

Winter is my favorite time of year—the only time we Angelenos experience any real change in the weather. As a native, there are few experiences more satisfying to me than cooking with the sound of a driving rain outside. Between showers the skies become brilliant blue with puffy clouds and one understands why so many have made this city their home. Polenta, gnocchi, baked pastas, and sauces that feature root vegetables take their turn on the menu.

Lasagna Bolognese

BOLOGNESE SAUCE, BÉCHAMEL, PARMESAN

Serves 6 to 8

OUR EVERYDAY BOLOGNESE SAUCE MAKES a special lasagna for wintry evenings when simply layered with tender egg pasta, béchamel sauce, and Parmesan.

8 TABLESPOONS (1 STICK) UNSALTED BUTTER

6 TABLESPOONS ALL-PURPOSE FLOUR

4 CUPS MILK

KOSHER SALT AND FRESHLY GROUND BLACK PEPPER TO TASTE

3 CUPS BOLOGNESE SAUCE (SEE PAGE 116)

1 RECIPE PASTA FRESCA ALL'UOVO (SEE PAGE 104), ROLLED OUT AND CUT INTO 13-INCH-LONG

SHEETS, OR 1 POUND FRESH PASTA SHEETS

1½ CUPS GRATED ITALIAN PARMESAN CHEESE FOR DUSTING

To make the béchamel, melt the butter in a small saucepan over low heat. Add the flour and stir to form a smooth paste. Meanwhile, heat the milk in a separate saucepan. When it is hot but not boiling, pour it into the roux (butter-flour mixture), stirring constantly with a whisk or a wooden spoon. Cook over low heat, stirring, until the sauce thickens and the floury taste is gone. Season with salt and pepper. Pour into a mixing bowl and set aside.

In a saucepan, heat the Bolognese sauce to a simmer, adding a bit of water to bring back its saucy quality. Set aside. Preheat the oven to 375°F. Lightly grease a 9 by 13-inch baking dish with butter. Cook the pasta in abundant boiling salted water until al dente; drain well.

Ladle just enough Bolognese sauce over the bottom of the baking dish to coat it lightly. Cover the sauce with a layer of lasagna noodles. Spoon a generous ladleful of béchamel sauce onto the pasta. Using a rubber spatula, spread it evenly. Generously dust Parmesan cheese over the béchamel. Top with another layer of pasta. Again make a generous layer of béchamel over the pasta, top the béchamel with the remaining Bolognese sauce, and dust liberally with Parmesan cheese. Top with a final layer of pasta and finish off with a layer of béchamel and Parmesan cheese. Cover with aluminum foil and bake for approximately 30 minutes, or until the lasagna is bubbling hot. Remove the foil for the last 10 minutes of cooking. Let sit for 10 minutes before serving.

Penne ai Tre Formaggi

RICOTTA, MASCARPONE, PARMESAN, WALNUTS

Serves 4 to 6

A WONDERFUL WOMAN NAMED KATHY TERNAY has worked at Angeli on and off for eight years. She combines her earthy Sicilian-Neapolitan roots with a love of light, elegant, and modern foods to produce some of the best that Angeli has to offer. This is one of her more recent contributions. Every time this dish appears as one of our daily specials, the staff prays that the kitchen makes too much, since leftover sauces are served at the end of the shift for the staff meal.

1 POUND RICOTTA CHEESE

4 OUNCES MASCARPONE CHEESE

1 CUP GRATED ITALIAN PARMESAN CHEESE, PLUS MORE FOR THE TABLE

10 FRESH BASIL LEAVES, COARSELY CHOPPED

KOSHER SALT AND FRESHLY GROUND BLACK PEPPER TO TASTE

1 POUND IMPORTED ITALIAN PENNE

1/2 CUP WALNUT PIECES, CHOPPED AND LIGHTLY TOASTED

Mix the ricotta, mascarpone, Parmesan, and basil together in a large serving bowl. Add salt and pepper to taste.

Cook the pasta in abundant boiling salted water until al dente. Just before draining the pasta, ladle out 1 cup of the pasta cooking water and add it to the cheese mixture in the serving bowl. Whisk the water into the cheese until smooth.

Quickly drain the pasta and place it in the serving bowl with the cheese mixture. Add the walnuts and toss to mix. Serve immediately with additional Parmesan cheese at the table.

Pasta Muro Leccese

TINY MEATBALLS, TOMATO SAUCE, ORECCHIETTE, GARLICKY BREAD CRUMBS

Serves 4 to 6

I'M FORTUNATE TO BELONG TO an organization called Oldways. Its mission is to preserve old ways, or traditions, of different food cultures. Occasionally I'm asked to go along on a special trip with them to explore the food resources of a particular area. A trip to the southern region of Puglia was a highlight of all my years spent traveling in Italy.

During my stay in the elegant baroque city of Lecce, an unusual package of pasta that was displayed in many store windows piqued my interest. Orecchiette were packaged together with the traditional Pugliese fusilli *fatto a mano* (shaped like ziti, but with tapered ends). To my delight, at a restaurant with the unlikely name of Sayonara, in the village of Muro Leccese, our group was presented with a large platter of these two "married" pastas tossed in this simple country sauce. I asked the woman chef/owner what the story behind the combined shapes was and she confirmed my hunch that it was an old traditional salute to the male and female—*"pasta maritata."* A characteristic of cucina Pugliese is the inventive use of bread crumbs. One often sees a simple sauce given additional nutritive value and more interesting texture with the addition of a handful of bread crumbs. Here we use our Angeli staple, garlicky bread crumbs.

FOR THE MEATBALLS

1 RUSSET POTATO

1/2 POUND GROUND CHICKEN

1/2 SMALL ONION, MINCED

2 GARLIC CLOVES, PEELED AND MINCED

1/2 CUP COARSELY CHOPPED FRESH ITALIAN PARSLEY

1/4 CUP GRATED PECORINO ROMANO CHEESE

1/4 CUP GRATED ITALIAN PARMESAN CHEESE

1 LARGE EGG, BEATEN

KOSHER SALT AND FRESHLY GROUND BLACK PEPPER TO TASTE

OLIVE OIL

One 28-ounce can Italian or Italian-style pear tomatoes with juice

¼ cup extra-virgin olive oil

4 garlic cloves, peeled

10 fresh basil leaves, coarsely chopped

Kosher salt and freshly ground black pepper to taste

½ cup Garlicky Bread Crumbs (see page 228)

½ pound imported Italian orecchiette

½ pound ziti, pasta al ceppo, or Pugliese fusilli fatto a mano

Grated Italian Parmesan cheese to taste, plus more for the table

To make the meatballs, place the potato in a small saucepan, cover with cold water, and bring to a boil. Cook until tender. Drain.

When the potato is cool enough to handle, peel it and put it through a potato ricer into a mixing bowl, or mash it thoroughly with a fork. Add the ground chicken, onion, garlic, parsley, Romano, Parmesan, egg, and salt and pepper to taste, and mix thoroughly but gently.

Lightly rub a bit of olive oil into the palm of your hand and make tiny meatballs, about the size of small olives. Don't worry about making them perfectly round, just make sure they are small. As you shape each meatball, place it on a lightly oiled cookie sheet or baking pan. Set aside.

Puree the tomatoes, with their juice, using the coarse disk of a food mill or in a food processor fitted with the steel blade. Set the puree aside.

Heat the oil with the garlic in a heavy saucepan. Cook the garlic until it is a deep golden brown, then remove the cloves from the pan and discard. Add the meatballs to the oil in the skillet. Sauté them over medium-high heat until they are well browned on all sides. Pour the tomato puree over the meatballs, being careful of splattering tomato sauce. Bring the sauce to a simmer. Add the basil and salt and pepper to taste. Cook over medium-high heat, stirring frequently, until the sauce thickens and the meatballs are tender but still juicy, about 40 minutes. Just before serving, stir the bread crumbs into the hot sauce.

Meanwhile, cook the orecchiette and ziti together in abundant boiling salted water until al dente. Carefully drain the pasta and place it in a serving bowl.

Add the Parmesan cheese and sauce and toss well to mix. Serve immediately, with additional Parmesan cheese at the table.

Gnocchi di Patate Ricca

POTATOES, BÉCHAMEL, FONTINA, PARMESAN

Serves 4 to 6

WHEN YOU MAKE THESE, test only one of the potatoes for doneness, and do not test too often, for each time it is pierced, it absorbs more water. To avoid adding too much flour to the dough, I always keep a small saucepan filled with simmering water on the stove so that I can test the mixture several times until I achieve the texture I want.

2 POUNDS RUSSET OR YELLOW FINNISH POTATOES

1 LARGE EGG, BEATEN

1 TO 2 CUPS ALL-PURPOSE FLOUR

1 TO 2 CUPS BÉCHAMEL SAUCE (SEE PAGE 222)

4 TABLESPOONS UNSALTED BUTTER

6 OUNCES ITALIAN FONTINA CHEESE, CUT INTO SMALL DICE

FRESHLY GROUND BLACK PEPPER TO TASTE

GRATED ITALIAN PARMESAN CHEESE TO TASTE

Place the potatoes, whole and unpeeled, in a saucepan with cold water to cover. Bring to a boil over high heat and cook until the potatoes are tender. Drain and peel them. Put the potatoes through a ricer into a medium mixing bowl and set aside until cool enough to handle.

Add the egg and 1 cup flour to the potatoes. Use your hand to mix in the egg and flour, kneading as you would a bread dough—but as little as possible. Too much mixing will toughen the gnocchi. The dough should be soft yet hold its shape; add up to 1 cup more flour if necessary (the amount depends on the humidity and on the type and age of the potatoes).

To form the gnocchi, break off pieces of dough as big as a child's fist. With floured hands, on a floured work surface, gently and quickly roll the dough into thick ropes about ¾ inch in diameter. Lay the cylinders on a floured board and, using a sharp knife, cut off pieces the width of a finger. As you turn the gnocchi lay them on a well-floured surface and make a small indentation in each dumpling with your thumb and forefinger. Take care to keep the dumplings apart to prevent them from sticking together. (You can place them in one layer on a cookie sheet and freeze at this point if you are not going cook them immediately. Once they are firm, transfer to plastic bags and freeze for up to 1 month.)

Preheat the oven to 375°F.

Bring a large pot of salted water to a boil. Turn the heat down so that the water simmers, and gently drop the gnocchi into the water. The gnocchi are done when they float to the surface. As the gnocchi are done, remove them with a slotted spoon, gently shaking off as much water as possible, and place them in a shallow ovenproof baking dish. Dot the gnocchi with the butter and scatter the Fontina cheese over them. Using a spoon, drop the béchamel in dollops over the gnocchi. Sprinkle with pepper and Parmesan cheese to taste.

Bake for approximately 20 minutes, or until the gnocchi are heated through and the cheese is melted and speckled with golden brown dots.

Ravioli al Val d'Aosta

FONTINA, PROSCIUTTO, PARSLEY, BÉCHAMEL

Serves 6 to 8

THIS RAVIOLI IS UNUSUAL IN THAT the filling becomes nearly like a fonduta, a Piedmontese sauce of Fontina, butter, milk, and egg yolks, as the heat of the boiling water causes the Fontina to melt into the béchamel. The bright flavor of white wine adds the final touch to the creamy cheese filling. The dish is presented drizzled with melted butter flavored with toasted walnuts and thyme, and a final dusting of Parmesan cheese adds its inviting aroma. A dish to eat in front of the fire when the weather is very cold—as a Californian, I can only dream.

FOR THE FILLING

3/4 POUND ITALIAN FONTINA CHEESE, GRATED

4 TO 5 SLICES PROSCIUTTO, MINCED

1/4 CUP MINCED FRESH ITALIAN PARSLEY

2 TABLESPOONS WHITE WINE

13/4 CUPS BÉCHAMEL SAUCE (SEE PAGE 222)

KOSHER SALT AND FRESHLY GROUND BLACK PEPPER TO TASTE

1 RECIPE PASTA FRESCA ALL'UOVO (SEE PAGE 104)

1 LARGE EGG, BEATEN, FOR EGG WASH

8 TABLESPOONS (1 STICK) UNSALTED BUTTER

1 CUP COARSELY CHOPPED TOASTED WALNUTS

2 SPRIGS THYME, LEAVES ONLY, PLUS WHOLE THYME SPRIGS FOR GARNISH

GRATED ITALIAN PARMESAN CHEESE FOR SPRINKLING

To make the filling, in a mixing bowl, stir together the Fontina, prosciutto, parsley, wine, and béchamel. Season with salt and pepper to taste.

To make the ravioli, using a pasta machine, roll out the dough through the thinnest setting, cutting it into sheets of manageable length as necessary. Do not roll out too many sheets at a time, or the dough will begin to dry out and become difficult to handle. Make a row of scant tablespoons of filling, 1 inch apart, just below the center of 1 pasta sheet. Brush beaten egg wash over all the borders. Carefully fold the sheet in half toward you, matching the horizontal edges of the dough. Gently press the pasta together around the mounds of filling to enclose it.

Using a pasta cutter-crimper, trim off the edges of the dough and cut apart the ravioli. Lay the ravioli on a lightly floured bedsheet or tea towels. Let dry at least 5 minutes before cooking.

Cook the ravioli in abundant boiling salted water until al dente; very fresh pasta only takes 2 to 5 minutes to cook. Lift the ravioli out of the boiling water with a slotted spoon or Chinese skimmer. Let the spoon or skimmer rest for a moment on a folded terry-cloth towel to absorb some of the cooking water, then gently lay the ravioli in a serving dish.

While the ravioli is cooking, melt the butter in a small skillet together with the walnuts and thyme leaves.

Pour the melted butter and walnuts over the ravioli in the serving dish. Sprinkle with Parmesan cheese and garnish with thyme sprigs.

Pizzocheri

SWISS CHARD, CABBAGE, POTATOES, FONTINA

Serves 4 to 6

BACK IN THE LATE SEVENTIES I spent quite a bit of time in the north of Italy. My memories of those trips are of youthful adventure interwoven with L'Unita festivals, the large, seemingly impromptu out-door carnivals put on by local Italian communist parties. Rough, local regional specialties were always in abundant supply at rock-bottom prices, a main draw for my friends and me, I'm sure, although the trancelike serenity produced by hours of two-stepping with gnarled old men had its exotic allure.

Pizzocheri is a staple of northern *cucina povera*. Few dishes are as humble in ingredients and rich in taste and satisfaction as this one is. At Angeli we always rush to make it during the one week or so of below-seventy-degree weather we have in Los Angeles. Be careful not to overcook the piz-zocheri; the buckwheat flour makes the noodles especially tender.

1 BUNCH SWISS CHARD

4 TABLESPOONS UNSALTED BUTTER

1 ONION, PEELED, CUT IN HALF LENGTHWISE, AND THINLY SLICED

1 TO 2 GARLIC CLOVES, PEELED AND SLICED

1/2 HEAD SAVOY CABBAGE, CUT INTO THIN SHREDS

KOSHER SALT AND FRESHLY GROUND BLACK PEPPER TO TASTE

1 POUND IMPORTED ITALIAN PIZZOCHERI

2 RUSSET POTATOES, BOILED, PEELED, AND CUT INTO 1/2-INCH DICE

1/2 POUND ITALIAN FONTINA CHEESE, DICED

GRATED ITALIAN PARMESAN CHEESE FOR DUSTING

Wash the chard well. Cut off the white ribs, trim them and cut into thin slices. Set aside. Stack the chard leaves, one atop the other, roll into a long cylinder, and cut into 1/2-inch-wide strips. Set aside.

Melt the butter in a large skillet. Add the onion and chard ribs and cook just until the chard is tender and the onion is becoming limp and sweet. Add the garlic and sauté until it releases its characteristic aroma. Add the cabbage and chard leaves and season with salt and pepper. Cover the pan and cook, stirring occasionally, until the cabbage and chard leaves are tender, approximately 10 minutes.

Meanwhile, cook the pizzocheri in abundant boiling salted water until al dente; just before the pasta is done, add the potatoes to heat them through.

Drain the pasta and potatoes and add to the skillet along with the Fontina cheese. Very gently toss the pasta with the vegetable mixture, then cover the pan and cook over low heat just until the cheese melts. Place the sauced pasta in individual pasta bowls and dust with Parmesan cheese. Serve immediately.

panini:
angeli to go

Angeli panini have developed quite a following over the past thirteen years. Despite the many imitations that can be found at local establishments, we are selling more now than ever. Made on Pane degli Angeli, Angeli bread, the sandwiches are big enough to satisfy the hungriest of diners.

No rustic Italian caffè or restaurant would be complete without bruschetta on the menu. Its primal simplicity has a prodigious ability to take away the edge of hunger while preparing the appetite for the dishes that follow.

Cicchetti and tramezzini make their appearance at our catered parties. Tramezzini, simple snack or tea sandwiches, are turned into elegant little bites in our kitchen, becoming a super-flavorful and more satisfying cousin of the stingy canapé. Cicchetti, a Venetian snack tradition, are perfectly suited to parties at an in-between hour, neither lunch nor dinner, when you wish to satisfy appetites while providing variety.

A large part of our business is carry-out. I suppose it was a natural evolution of our service, sitting as we do in the middle of the world's largest concentration of television and film production and postproduction facilities. Many of our regular customers who are in "the business" want Angeli food delivered to their writing and production staffs or assembled cast members. We are fortunate to be able to provide the meals for many video and commercial shoots that occur daily on the stages and streets of Los Angeles. Demand for corporate lunches and at-home dinners for the couch potatoes among us who want to coddle themselves challenges us to concoct tasty dishes that travel well.

Good food can often be the difference, during a grueling workday or burnt-out evening, between good-humored productivity and grumpiness. In addition, our weather lends itself to casually improvised outdoor meals nearly year-round. So we do our best to keep our clientele happy with a large repertoire of dishes that travel well and are impressive to serve.

a word about bread

It is easy for me, living as I do in Los Angeles, to simply pick up a wonderful crusty boule from La Brea Bakery, a ciabatta from Il Fornaio, or an herb-flecked loaf from La Buona Forchetta. However, I'm certainly aware that resources vary from community to community—some will have many high-quality European-style breads available, while others have very meager offerings.

Good peasant bread lasts quite a long time. Many recipes are based on those baked in centuries past in community ovens, resulting in loaves that had to keep a family going for many days or even a couple of weeks. The mouth learned to prize the crumb of the bread at its different stages, and the idea of bread going stale was more one of "aging." Most country Italian and French loaves are made from natural starters, which provide a deep moistness to the crumb of a loaf. The crust, in turn, is very hard, protecting the inside for a long, long time.

On a recent trip to Italy, a friend, Ari Weinzweig, brought along an Italian peasant bread from his bakery, Zingerman's Bakehouse, in Ann Arbor, Michigan, as an experiment. We shared a rental car for about ten days and that bread was as good on the last day of the trip, as we rooted about for a hardened bit of crust, as it was on the first day, fragrant with yeasty moistness. It was on that trip that I became a convert to the idea that ordering bread by mail from a superlative supplier is not only possible but preferable if the local choices are dismal enough.

Most of the panini recipes are at their best served, of course, on Angeli bread (see page 95) or on a traditional hard-crusted, firm-crumbed Italian or French peasant loaf. The bruschetta should be made only on a bread of sturdy crumb. Conversely, many of the cicchetti are delicious on a soft bun made with milk and/or butter in the dough or even with the famous Italian roll, the *michette*, which is almost all crust, being nearly totally hollow. Some suggested breads to use for the tramezzini are white, egg, multigrain, pumpernickel, potato-dill, and walnut. The crumb should be uniform with no large holes in it and fairly soft to the bite. Follow your mouth and your nose until you create the combinations best suited to your palate.

panini

Panini are the prototypical Italian between-meal, on-the-run snack, to be enjoyed standing up or leaning at a chest-high table and usually followed by a quick shot of heart-throbbing espresso. In all my years of eating my way through Italy, I have never seen panini offered as part of a restaurant lunch menu. They are relegated to bars, *paninoteche* (sandwich bars, but these are still a rarity), and a few stylish caffès. Somehow it should come as no surprise that a people who believe heart and soul in the seriousness of satisfying the appetite relish snack time as much as any other meal. For us a sandwich is a meal, but for an Italian it is often just a snack, eaten when one is alone and running from one appointment to another.

Across the ocean, sandwiches are an American institution. They are a part of our eating tradition that has always been expressed with baroque flair (think Dagwood) and with less puritanical guilt than other meals. Even the most upscale or formal of our modern dining establishments include sandwiches on the lunch menu.

Angeli presents panini as a fusion of the generous American sandwich tradition and the Italian palette of flavors, ingredients, and presentation.

Panino Angeli

EGGPLANT, TOMATO, FRESH MOZZARELLA, BASIL

Makes 1 panino

OUR MOST POPULAR PANINO. Make this sandwich during the summer when fresh ripe tomatoes, sweet creamy eggplants, and fragrant basil can be found easily in produce markets. I love to experiment with the taste of the sandwich by trying different varieties of tomatoes and basil. My favorite combination is the Carmello tomato and the large-leafed, slightly ruffled *basilico napoletano*. The tomatoes are large and juicy with a beautiful balance of sugar and acid; the basil leaves are as big as small lettuce leaves, ensuring that you taste basil in every bite of the sandwich. It isn't important to search the earth for these particular varieties—what *is* important is to make the commitment to support local growers through neighborhood farmers' markets.

1 SMALL FIRM SHINY EGGPLANT, ENDS TRIMMED, PEELED, AND CUT INTO $\frac{1}{4}$-INCH-THICK SLICES

KOSHER SALT

EXTRA-VIRGIN OLIVE OIL

BREAD OR ROLL OF YOUR CHOICE

1 SMALL VINE-RIPENED TOMATO, SLICED

2 OUNCES FRESH MOZZARELLA, DRAINED AND CUT INTO THICK SLICES

FRESH BASIL LEAVES

FRESHLY GROUND BLACK PEPPER TO TASTE

Lay the eggplant out in one layer on paper towels. Sprinkle generously with salt and let sit until the bitter juices in the eggplant bead up on the eggplant's cut surfaces, about 30 minutes. Pat the eggplant dry with clean paper towels, rubbing off the salt as well. (If you can find eggplant that is young, firm, and with few seeds, it probably will not need this treatment.)

Heat a charcoal or gas grill or ridged stovetop griddle, or preheat the broiler. Grill or broil the eggplant slices on both sides until tender, brushing the slices with olive oil as they cook to provide flavor and to soften the sweet flesh.

To assemble the sandwich, drizzle both slices of bread or the roll with your favorite extra-virgin olive oil. Make a layer of the tomato slices, then top with the mozzarella. Arrange a few slices of the grilled eggplant atop the mozzarella. (You will have too much eggplant for one sandwich, so save the extra for another use.) Finish the panino with a layer of fresh basil leaves. Add a sprinkle of salt and a grind of black pepper. Place the top slice of bread or the top of the roll on the sandwich and cut in half for easier eating. Serve with lots of paper napkins.

Panino Verdura

GRILLED VEGETABLES, FENNEL, RICOTTA SALATA

Makes 4 panini

THE PREPARATION FOR THESE PANINI may seem like a lot of work, but all of it can be done in advance. Each of the vegetables adds its distinct flavor, texture, and color to create a combination that needs no additional herbs or condiments. Sometimes I roast rather than grill the peppers for a change. Ricotta salata is a simple farm cheese produced by salting fresh ricotta, setting it in a mold, and aging it for a brief period of time. Pungent yet creamy, it adds interest to salads, pasta dishes, and panini. It gives this sandwich a creamy bite and prevents the overall taste from being too sweet.

2 JAPANESE EGGPLANTS, ENDS TRIMMED, SLICED ON THE DIAGONAL INTO $1/4$-INCH-THICK SLICES

KOSHER SALT

2 FENNEL BULBS, TOUGH OUTER LEAVES AND WOODY CORES DISCARDED

2 TABLESPOONS OLIVE OIL, PLUS ADDITIONAL FOR GRILLING

FRESHLY GROUND BLACK PEPPER TO TASTE

2 RED OR YELLOW BELL PEPPERS, CUT IN HALF LENGTHWISE, AND STEMS, SEEDS, AND TOUGH WHITE RIBS REMOVED

2 SMALL FIRM ZUCCHINI, ENDS TRIMMED AND CUT LENGTHWISE INTO $1/4$-INCH-THICK SLICES

1 RED ONION, PEELED AND CUT CROSSWISE INTO THICK SLICES

BREAD OR ROLLS OF YOUR CHOICE

RICOTTA SALATA CHEESE TO TASTE

EXTRA-VIRGIN OLIVE OIL FOR DRIZZLING

Lay the eggplant out in one layer on paper towels. Sprinkle generously with salt and let sit until the bitter juices bead up on the eggplant's cut surfaces, about 30 minutes. Pat the eggplant dry with clean paper towels, rubbing off the salt as well. (If the eggplant is young, firm, and without seeds, it probably will not need this treatment.)

Meanwhile, cut the fennel bulbs in half lengthwise. Put the cut sides facedown on your cutting board and cut the bulbs into thin crosswise slices. In a large skillet, sauté the fennel slices in the olive oil over medium heat until they soften. Season with salt and pepper to taste. Set aside while you prepare the other vegetables.

Heat a charcoal or gas grill or a ridged stovetop griddle, or preheat the broiler. Grill or broil the eggplant, peppers, zucchini, and onion slices on both sides, brushing the slices with olive oil as they cook to provide flavor and to soften the sweet flesh. As each vegetable softens to the texture you like, remove it from the grill to a platter. When all the vegetables are cooked, sprinkle salt and pepper to taste over them.

Arrange the grilled vegetables on half of the bread or the bottoms of the rolls. Top with the sautéed fennel. Using the large holes of a box grater, grate ricotta salata to taste over each sandwich. Drizzle a bit of extra-virgin olive oil over all. Place a second slice of bread or the top of the roll on each sandwich, cut in half, and serve.

Panino di Frittata con Peperonata

HERB FRITTATA, PEPERONATA

Makes 4 panini

WHEN SERVING FRITTATA AS A MAIN DISH, we often make them so big and tall that they are nearly egg cakes. However, for panini, it serves to make the more traditional thin frittata, about three quarters of an inch thick. There are few tastes as well suited to each other as eggs and peperonata, a classic antipasto with its characteristic *agrodolce* flavors. I prefer the peperonata with a bit of chill on it from the refrigerator, so I usually make it at least one day ahead. The flavors mellow and become more complex as it sits.

FOR THE PEPERONATA

4 GARLIC CLOVES, PEELED AND MINCED

1/2 RED ONION, PEELED AND COARSELY CHOPPED

1/4 CUP EXTRA-VIRGIN OLIVE OIL

2 RED BELL PEPPERS, CUT IN HALF LENGTHWISE, STEMS, SEEDS, AND TOUGH WHITE RIBS
REMOVED, AND CUT INTO 1/2-INCH-WIDE STRIPS

1/4 CUP RED WINE VINEGAR

3 ROMA TOMATOES, PEELED, SEEDED, AND COARSELY CHOPPED

1 TO 3 TABLESPOONS SUGAR

KOSHER SALT TO TASTE

FOR THE FRITTATA

8 LARGE EGGS

1/2 CUP GRATED ITALIAN PARMESAN CHEESE

3/4 CUP FINELY CHOPPED MIXED HERBS OF YOUR CHOICE

KOSHER SALT AND FRESHLY GROUND BLACK PEPPER TO TASTE

1/4 CUP EXTRA-VIRGIN OLIVE OIL

BREAD OR ROLLS OF YOUR CHOICE

To make the peperonata, sauté the garlic and onion in the oil in a large skillet over medium heat until the onion begins to soften. Add the peppers and sauté gently, stirring frequently, until they are soft. Add the vinegar and cook, covered, for about 3 minutes. Add the tomatoes and cook, uncovered, until they give off their juices and the mixture begins to thicken. Add enough sugar so you have a pleasing sweet-sour taste, then add salt to taste. Set the peperonata in a bowl to cool.

To make the frittata, in a mixing bowl, beat together the eggs, cheese, and herbs. Add salt and pepper to taste. Heat the oil in a 12-inch nonstick skillet with sloping sides. Swirl the oil in the pan to coat the sides. Pour in the eggs and lower the heat. Cook, stirring frequently, until the eggs have formed small curds and the frittata is firm except for the top. To cook the top, you can turn the frittata over by sliding it out of the pan onto a large plate, then flipping it over back into the pan. Or you can lightly brown the top under the broiler. (Or simply cover it for a while with a lid until it achieves the desired firmness.) When the frittata is done, carefully slide it out of the pan onto a cutting board or plate.

To assemble the panini, drizzle a bit of the juices from the peperonata onto half the bread or the bottom of the rolls. Cut the frittata into wedges and place on the bread or rolls. Spoon on the peperonata and top with the remaining bread or the roll tops. Serve with lots of napkins. Good and messy!

Rustico

ICKEN SALAD, ARUGULA

ini

ONE DAY MY FORMER PARTNER, John Strobel, decided to put our chicken salad on Angeli bread with arugula and Dijon mustard. A new favorite was born—some days our chefs wish we had a machine that could pump these out automatically. Use a sturdy roll with a hard crust for this panino, as the juice from the chicken salad will permeate the bread.

4 BONELESS CHICKEN BREASTS, SKIN ON

KOSHER SALT AND FRESHLY GROUND BLACK PEPPER TO TASTE

1 LEMON

1/2 CUP EXTRA-VIRGIN OLIVE OIL

1/4 CUP BALSAMIC VINEGAR

2 TABLESPOONS TOASTED PINE NUTS

1 TABLESPOON RAISINS, PLUMPED IN HOT WATER FOR 10 MINUTES, THEN DRAINED (OPTIONAL)

ROLLS OF YOUR CHOICE

DIJON MUSTARD

SMALL BUNCH OF ARUGULA, STEMS TRIMMED, WASHED, AND DRIED

Preheat the oven to 400°F.

Place the chicken on a baking sheet, skin side up. Bake for about 15 minutes, or until cooked through. Remove from the oven and let cool.

When the chicken has cooled, remove and discard the skin. Shred the meat and place in a medium stainless or glass bowl. Add salt and pepper to taste. Use a citrus zester to zest the lemon directly over the shredded chicken. Cut the zested lemon in half and squeeze the juice from one half over the chicken. Add the olive oil, balsamic vinegar, pine nuts, and the raisins if desired. Stir gently to mix.

To assemble the panini, slather the bottom of a roll with Dijon mustard. Spoon the chicken salad and some of the juices onto the rolls and top with the arugula and the tops of the rolls. Cut in half and serve.

Panino di Portobello

BABY SPINACH, PORTOBELLO MUSHROOMS, SWEET RED PEPPERS, PARMESAN

Makes 4 panini

ONE OF THE PLEASURES OF RESTAURANT cooking is that beautiful ingredients find their way to you with very little effort on your part. We love to experiment with baby greens of the season and are lucky to have a local grower who has ready supplies of mizuna, tatsoi, and baby mustard greens, as well as the more common baby spinach and rapini.

1 POUND TENDER BABY SPINACH OR OTHER BABY GREENS, WELL WASHED

1 SMALL BUNCH FRESH THYME, LEAVES ONLY, FINELY CHOPPED

4 GARLIC CLOVES, PEELED AND MINCED

4 LARGE PORTOBELLO MUSHROOMS, STEMS REMOVED AND WIPED CLEAN

2 RED BELL PEPPERS, CUT IN HALF LENGTHWISE, AND STEMS, SEEDS, AND TOUGH WHITE RIBS REMOVED

EXTRA-VIRGIN OLIVE OIL

KOSHER SALT AND FRESHLY GROUND BLACK PEPPER TO TASTE

BREAD OR ROLLS OF YOUR CHOICE

4 OUNCES ITALIAN PARMESAN CHEESE, SHAVED OR GRATED

Put the spinach in a saucepan with just the water clinging to its leaves, add a pinch of salt, cover, and cook over medium heat just until tender. Drain well and set aside.

Heat a charcoal or gas grill or preheat the oven to 400°F.

Mix together the chopped thyme and garlic in a small bowl. Stuff the herb mixture into the black gills on the underside of the mushroom caps. Brush the mushrooms and bell peppers with olive oil and sprinkle with salt and pepper to taste. Place on the hot grill or in the preheated oven and cook, turning occasionally, until the mushrooms are tender and the peppers are nicely charred and have begun to soften. Transfer to a platter.

To make the panini, drizzle the olive oil over the slices of bread or the rolls. Layer the braised greens, mushrooms, and peppers on half of the bread or the bottoms of the rolls. Top with the Parmesan cheese and the remaining bread or the tops of the rolls. Cut in half and serve.

Panino Grosso

MIXED ITALIAN MEATS AND CHEESES

Makes 4 panini

MUFFULETTA, HERO, AND SUBMARINE are just a few of the many variations on the Italian sandwich-with-everything theme. We call ours a *panino grosso*; *grosso* means big in Italian (not gross!). This is one of those sandwiches that travels really well. The juices from all the condiments and the dressing mix with the meats and the bread so the panino becomes almost like a savory tart. Great picnic food.

GARLIC-PARMESAN DRESSING (SEE PAGE 224) FOR DRIZZLING

BREAD OR ROLLS OF YOUR CHOICE

8 THIN SLICES MORTADELLA

12 THIN SLICES CAPPICOLA

8 THIN SLICES SOPPRESSATA

12 THIN SLICES SALAME TOSCANO

16 THIN SLICES PROVOLONE CHEESE

RED ONION CONDIMENT (SEE PAGE 222) FOR GARNISH

ROASTED PEPPER–OLIVE CONDIMENT (SEE PAGE 223) FOR GARNISH

Drizzle the garlic dressing to taste over the slices of bread or the rolls. Arrange the meats and cheese on half the bread or the bottoms of the rolls. Top with both condiments to taste. Cover with the remaining bread or the tops of the rolls. Serve with lots of napkins.

Panino Sarno

RAPINI, SAUSAGES, PECORINO ROMANO

Makes 4 panini

RAPINI, OR BROCCOLI RABE, is a green described as *amarolo,* or slightly bitter, by Italians. As with its slightly bitter cousins, radicchio, endive, and escarole, you either love the distinct character of the subtle bitterness or you don't. For those who do, rapini tends to be an addiction. I can never make this panino without thinking of my close friends Lydia and Maria Sarno, who were brought up on this vitamin-rich earthy green. Blanching the rapini tones down the bitterness, but always taste a bit of it raw first—it may be subtle enough not to need blanching. For a vegetarian meal, simply braise the rapini in a bit more olive oil and omit the sausage.

> 1 BUNCH RAPINI (BROCCOLI RABE), STEMS TRIMMED AND WASHED
>
> 2 TEASPOONS KOSHER SALT, PLUS MORE TO TASTE
>
> 2 SWEET ITALIAN SAUSAGES, CASINGS REMOVED
>
> 2 TABLESPOONS OLIVE OIL
>
> 2 TO 4 GARLIC CLOVES, PEELED AND SLICED
>
> PINCH OF RED CHILE PEPPER FLAKES
>
> BREAD OR ROLLS OF YOUR CHOICE
>
> GRATED IMPORTED PECORINO ROMANO CHEESE (OPTIONAL)

Bring a large pot of water to the boil. Add the rapini and salt. Blanch the rapini for 5 minutes, drain, and set aside while you cook the sausages.

In a large skillet, sauté the sausage meat in the olive oil over medium heat, breaking up the meat, until no trace of pink remains. Transfer the sausage meat to a plate and drain the pan of all but 2 tablespoons of fat. Add the garlic and red pepper flakes to the pan and sauté just until the garlic is fragrant. Add the rapini, 1/4 cup water, and cooked sausage meat, cover the pan, and braise until the greens are tender, about 5 minutes. (This mixture can be made several days ahead and refrigerated. It is equally delicious hot or cold.)

To assemble the panini, divide the rapini-sausage mixture among half the bread or the bottoms of the rolls. Sprinkle with a bit of Pecorino Romano cheese if desired, and cover with the remaining bread or tops of the rolls.

Panino McAngeli

EGGS, CHEESE, PROSCIUTTO

Makes 4 panini

IN A CITY THAT HAS AT least two McDonald's in every neighborhood, it was inevitable that a breakfast catering client would want this sandwich. I turned up my nose at the request at first—that is, until I tasted the combination myself. It's the kind of sandwich that plays into every comfort fantasy we have as well as satisfying the occasional desire to "cheat"—cholesterol, pork, salt, cheese—what could be better! Some people feel that they must add a grilled tomato just to feel a bit more healthy. I prefer it hard-core, but try it when tomatoes are in season. This is a great sandwich to make for kids' breakfasts.

4 TABLESPOONS UNSALTED BUTTER

4 LARGE EGGS

KOSHER SALT AND FRESHLY GROUND BLACK PEPPER TO TASTE

4 SLICES CHEESE OF YOUR CHOICE: CHEDDAR, PROVOLONE, PARMESAN, SWISS

BREAD OR ROLLS OF YOUR CHOICE

8 THIN SLICES PROSCIUTTO

Melt the butter in a nonstick skillet over medium heat. Cook the eggs to your preference: fried, over-easy, hard, or scrambled; they all work well in this sandwich. Add salt and pepper to taste.

While the eggs are cooking, place the cheese on half the bread or the tops of the rolls and place in a toaster oven or under a hot broiler until the cheese melts; heat the remaining bread or the bottoms of the rolls as well.

As soon as the eggs are done, remove them from the skillet to the plain slices of bread or the roll bottoms. Top each with 2 slices prosciutto and with the bread or roll tops with the melted cheese. Cut in half and enjoy.

Panino alla Porchetta

FENNEL-INFUSED PORK ROAST, FENNEL, SAGE

Makes 6 panini

IF YOU CAN'T FIND A SMALL PORK ROAST, buy a large one, double the amount of "paste" ingredients, and eat a fabulous *arista* (roast pork) dinner accompanied by sage-roasted potatoes. Then use the leftover pork roast to make this satisfying sandwich.

FOR THE PORK ROAST

3 GARLIC CLOVES, PEELED AND MINCED

2 TEASPOONS FENNEL SEEDS

1/4 CUP CHOPPED RESERVED FRESH FENNEL TOPS (SEE BELOW)

1 SPRIG ROSEMARY, LEAVES ONLY, FINELY CHOPPED

1 TO 2 TEASPOONS KOSHER SALT, PLUS MORE TO TASTE

FRESHLY GROUND BLACK PEPPER TO TASTE

ONE 2-POUND BONELESS PORK RIB ROAST

EXTRA-VIRGIN OLIVE OIL

2 FENNEL BULBS, TOUGH OUTER LEAVES REMOVED, HALVED, CORED, AND THINLY SLICED CROSSWISE, FENNEL TOPS RESERVED

3/4 CUP OLIVE OIL

KOSHER SALT AND COARSELY GROUND BLACK PEPPER TO TASTE

SMALL BUNCH OF SAGE, LEAVES ONLY

BREAD OR ROLLS OF YOUR CHOICE

Preheat the oven to 350°F.

Combine the minced garlic, fennel seeds, fennel tops, rosemary, salt, and pepper to taste in a mortar and pound to a paste with the pestle, or chop and mash with the side of a chef's knife. If the roast is already rolled and tied, unroll it. Spread most of the paste over the meat, reserving a tablespoon or so. Roll and tie the roast so that the pale tenderloin is more or less in the center, surrounded by the darker meat of the loin. With a sharp knife, make a few incisions about ½ inch deep in the roast and stuff some of the paste into them. Rub any remaining paste over the outside of the meat. Rub a little extra-virgin olive oil over the meat and place in a roasting pan.

Roast the pork, uncovered, for about 1¼ hours, or until the internal temperature registers 155–160° on a meat thermometer. Baste the roast two or three times with the pan juices. Remove the roast from the oven and allow to cool.

In a large skillet, sauté the fennel slices in ¼ cup of the olive oil over low heat until very tender. Season with salt and pepper to taste. Set aside.

Heat the remaining ½ cup olive oil in a small skillet, and fry the sage leaves until crisp.

To prepare the sandwiches, cut the roast into ¼-inch-thick slices and bathe them in the pan juices. Lift the meat out of the juices and place on half the bread or the bottoms of the rolls. Top with the sautéed fennel, crisp sage leaves, and the remaining bread or tops of the rolls.

Panino di Pasqua

ROAST LAMB, EGGPLANT, SWEET RED PEPPERS

Makes 6 panini

A WHOLE BONELESS LEG OF LAMB will yield enough thinly sliced meat for ten sandwiches. Since it is nearly impossible to find a smaller roast, plan these panini for when a crowd is coming. Or cook a roast for an intimate dinner and use the remaining meat for sandwiches.

3 GARLIC CLOVES, PEELED AND MINCED

3 TO 4 SPRIGS ROSEMARY, LEAVES ONLY, FINELY CHOPPED

1 TO 2 TEASPOONS KOSHER SALT

2 POUNDS BONELESS LEG OF LAMB

OLIVE OIL

2 JAPANESE EGGPLANTS, ENDS TRIMMED, PEELED, AND CUT LENGTHWISE INTO ¼-INCH-THICK SLICES

2 RED BELL PEPPERS OR 2 JARRED ROASTED RED PEPPERS

2 TABLESPOONS EXTRA-VIRGIN OLIVE OIL, PLUS ADDITIONAL IF NECESSARY

GARLIC MAYONNAISE (SEE PAGE 227)

BREAD OR ROLLS OF YOUR CHOICE

CONTINUED

Preheat the oven to 325°F.

Mash the garlic, rosemary, and salt to a paste by chopping them together with a chef's knife. If the roast is rolled and tied, unroll it. Spread most of the paste over the meat, reserving a tablespoon or so. Roll and tie the roast, using kitchen twine if necessary. Make a few incisions with a sharp knife about ½ inch deep in the roast and stuff some of the paste into them. Rub any remaining paste over the outside of the meat. Rub a little olive oil over the meat and place it in a roasting pan.

Roast, uncovered, for about 2 hours, or until the internal temperature registers 165°F on a meat thermometer. Baste the roast two or three times with the pan juices. Remove the roast from the oven and allow to cool for several minutes before slicing.

While the lamb is roasting, prepare the eggplant and peppers. Heat the extra-virgin olive oil in a large nonstick frying pan over high heat. Sauté the eggplant slices, in batches, until they are golden brown on both sides and quite tender, adding more oil to the pan as necessary. Remove from the pan with tongs and drain on paper towels.

If using fresh peppers, roast them over a gas flame, under the broiler, or in the oven, turning occasionally, until they are completely charred. Immediately place them in a plastic bag and twist the bag closed tight (the resulting steam from the hot peppers will soften the charred skin). After about 15 minutes, remove the peppers from the bag and carefully rub off the charred skins. Pull out the stem and discard the seeds; if necessary, trim any tough white ribs. Slice into strips. Set aside on a small plate.

To assemble the panini, slice the lamb as thin as you can. Slather the garlic mayonnaise over half the slices of bread. Layer the sliced lamb, eggplant, and roasted peppers on top, and top with the remaining bread. Cut in half before serving.

Panino di Carne Balsamico

ROSEMARY-BALSAMIC FLANK STEAK, WATERCRESS

Makes 6 panini

FLANK STEAK ABSORBS THE SWEET SHARPNESS of the marinade so that upon grilling, its fibers are saturated with flavor. Let the meat sit for a few minutes before cutting to allow the steak to keep more of its luscious juices. The bite of whole-grain mustard and horseradish mayonnaise mixes with the crunch of fresh arugula to create an absolutely delicious panino.

1 CUP BALSAMIC VINEGAR

1 TEASPOON DIJON MUSTARD

2 SPRIGS ROSEMARY, LEAVES ONLY, FINELY CHOPPED

2 GARLIC CLOVES, PEELED AND CRUSHED

KOSHER SALT AND FRESHLY GROUND BLACK PEPPER TO TASTE

1 FLANK STEAK (ABOUT 2 POUNDS)

WHOLE-GRAIN MUSTARD (OPTIONAL)

BREAD OR ROLLS OF YOUR CHOICE

1 BUNCH WATERCRESS, STEMS TRIMMED, WELL WASHED, AND DRIED

HORSERADISH MAYONNAISE (SEE PAGE 226)

Combine the vinegar, mustard, rosemary, garlic, and salt and pepper to taste in a shallow dish just large enough to hold the flank steak. Put the meat in the marinade, turning it a few times to completely bathe it in the flavorings. Cover the meat with plastic wrap, refrigerate and let it marinate from 2 hours to overnight, turning the meat occasionally.

Heat a charcoal or gas grill or preheat the broiler. Remove the meat from the marinade, reserving the marinade. Grill or broil, basting a few times with the marinade, for about 4 minutes on each side, or until the meat is medium-rare. Transfer the meat to a plate and let rest for a few minutes. (The meat can be cooked up to 1 day ahead if desired and refrigerated.)

Meanwhile, pour the reserved marinade into a small saucepan and bring to a boil. Boil for 1 minute, then remove from the heat and set aside.

To make the sandwiches, thinly slice the meat on an extreme diagonal angle across the grain of the meat (to avoid toughness); reserve any meat juices that have accumulated on the plate. Drizzle the slices of meat with a bit of the reserved marinade.

Spread a bit of mustard if you desire on half the bread or the bottom halves of the rolls. Top with the meat and watercress. Drizzle a tablespoonful or so of the reserved meat juices over the watercress. Spread the horseradish mayonnaise on the remaining bread or the tops of the rolls, put atop the panini, cut in half, and serve.

Panino Tagliata

ROSEMARY, SAGE, BEEF FILLET, ARUGULA, GRILLED TOMATO
Makes 4 panini

IN THE EARLY EIGHTIES MY "SISTER" CAROL lived in Milan and I spent a few weeks of every year there. La Libera in the Brera district was a favorite bistro. I had a *secondo* there that was a revelation to me at the time. Called *tagliata,* which means "cut," it was simply thin scallops of beef tenderloin seared so quickly it was almost a cooked carpaccio. The scallops were arranged atop a bed of arugula and topped with fresh sage and rosemary. At Angeli we served that dish as an entrée with great success for many years before it occurred to us to turn it into a sandwich as well. It's very messy but worth it. If you find cutting and cooking the tenderloin to be too much trouble, substitute very rare deli roast beef.

2 SPRIGS ROSEMARY, LEAVES ONLY, MINCED

8 FRESH SAGE LEAVES, MINCED

1 POUND BEEF TENDERLOIN, TRIMMED OF ALL FAT AND SINEW

1/2 CUP SOUR CREAM

1/4 CUP BUTTERMILK

1 TABLESPOON DIJON MUSTARD

KOSHER SALT AND FRESHLY GROUND BLACK PEPPER TO TASTE

2 BUNCHES ARUGULA, STEMS TRIMMED, WASHED, AND DRIED

BREAD OR ROLLS OF YOUR CHOICE

BALSAMIC VINEGAR FOR DRIZZLING

4 ROMA TOMATOES, CUT IN HALF LENGTHWISE

Mix the chopped herbs together in a small bowl and set aside.

Cut the beef into 4 medallions and place between two pieces of wax paper. Pound the medallions gently until they are approximately ¼ inch thick. Sprinkle the herbs over the scallops and set them aside.

In a small bowl, mix together the sour cream, buttermilk, mustard, and salt and pepper to taste. Set aside so the flavors can mix.

Arrange the arugula on half the bread or the bottoms of the rolls, drizzle with balsamic vinegar, and set aside.

Heat a griddle or large cast-iron skillet over high heat. Lightly oil the griddle or skillet using an oiled paper towel. Place the tomatoes cut side down on the griddle and cook, turning once, until they soften and are lightly charred on both sides. Remove from the heat and set aside.

Lightly oil the pan again if necessary. Working quickly, sear the beef scallops briefly, so that they are still very rare. As the beef scallops are done, remove them from the heat and immediately place atop the arugula, distributing them evenly among the bread. Top the meat with the charred tomatoes. Finish by drizzling with the sour cream dressing and topping with the remaining bread or the tops of the rolls.

Panino Tonno alla Griglia con Finocchio

FENNEL, RED ONION, CAPERS, GRILLED TUNA, WATERCRESS

Makes 4 panini

THE SWEETNESS OF THE ONION and fennel acts as an excellent foil for the meaty flavor of this tuna. The capers and parsley add piquant sharpness for contrast. This panino is best presented open-faced, the tuna topped with the onion-fennel mixture on one slice of bread and a few watercress sprigs atop the other slice.

2 TO 4 TABLESPOONS OLIVE OIL (TO TASTE)

1 FENNEL BULB, TRIMMED OF TOUGH OUTER LAYERS, CORED, AND CUT INTO THIN CROSSWISE SLICES, FEATHERY TOPS RESERVED AND CHOPPED

1 SMALL RED ONION, PEELED AND CUT CROSSWISE INTO THIN SLICES

1 TEASPOON CAPERS, RINSED

1/4 CUP CHOPPED FRESH ITALIAN PARSLEY

4 TUNA STEAKS, ABOUT 1/2 INCH THICK

OLIVE OIL FOR GRILLING

KOSHER SALT AND FRESHLY GROUND BLACK PEPPER TO TASTE

BREAD OR ROLLS OF YOUR CHOICE

1 BUNCH WATERCRESS, STEMS TRIMMED, WASHED, AND DRIED

OLIVE MAYONNAISE (SEE PAGE 227) (OPTIONAL)

Place the olive oil, fennel, and red onion in a small sauté pan and cook over medium heat until the fennel and onion are very tender. Add the capers, parsley, and chopped fennel tops and cook for 3 more minutes. Spoon the mixture into a small bowl and set aside while you cook the fish.

Heat a charcoal or gas grill or ridged stovetop griddle until very hot, or preheat the broiler. Lightly rub the grill with an oiled towel to prevent the fish from sticking. Brush each tuna steak with a bit of oil and sprinkle with salt and pepper to taste. Grill or broil for approximately 3 minutes per side, or until the fish feels firm when pressed with your finger.

To assemble the panini, place a slice of bread or the bottom of a roll on each plate. Lay the tuna steaks atop the bread, and top with the fennel mixture. Lay the remaining bread or the tops of the rolls alongside and garnish with watercress. If desired place a small ramekin of olive mayonnaise on each plate. Serve immediately.

Panino di Pesce Spada

YELLOW PEPPERS, SWORDFISH

Makes 4 panini

SUPER-FRESH LINE-CAUGHT SWORDFISH IS a treat when cut thin and quickly grilled, and serving it in a panino means that none of the succulent juices will be lost.

2 YELLOW BELL PEPPERS, CUT IN HALF LENGTHWISE, STEMS, SEEDS, AND TOUGH WHITE RIBS REMOVED, AND CUT INTO $1/4$-INCH STRIPS

2 TABLESPOONS EXTRA-VIRGIN OLIVE OIL, PLUS ADDITIONAL TO TASTE

3 SPRIGS THYME OR $1/4$ TEASPOON DRIED THYME LEAVES

KOSHER SALT TO TASTE

OLIVE OIL FOR GRILLING

4 SWORDFISH STEAKS, $1/2$ INCH THICK

BREAD OR ROLLS OF YOUR CHOICE

PIQUANT MAYONNAISE (SEE PAGE 226), TO TASTE

4 RED-LEAF LETTUCE LEAVES FOR GARNISH

LEMON WEDGES

Place the bell peppers, oil, and thyme in a large skillet and cook, covered, over medium heat for about 5 minutes, or until the peppers begin to wilt, stirring occasionally. Remove the lid and continue to cook until the juices begin to evaporate. Add salt to taste and lower the heat. Sauté the peppers until they are dotted with bits of golden color and sweet, adding more olive oil to the pan if desired. When the peppers are done, remove the thyme sprigs if you use them and discard.

Heat a charcoal or gas grill or ridged stovetop griddle until very hot, or preheat the broiler. Lightly rub the grill with an oiled paper towel to prevent the fish from sticking. Brush each swordfish steak with a bit of oil and sprinkle with salt and pepper. Grill or broil the fish for 3 minutes per side, or until the fish feels firm when pressed with a finger and is cooked all the way through.

To assemble the panini, place 2 slices of bread alongside each other on each plate, and lay a cooked swordfish steak atop one slice. Top each piece of swordfish with a dollop of piquant mayonnaise. Garnish the remaining slices of bread with the lettuce leaves and the yellow peppers. Serve open-faced, accompanied by lemon wedges.

Panino alle Moleche

SOFT-SHELL CRAB, TOMATO, BASIL

Makes 4 panini

SOFT-SHELL CRABS ARE BLUE CRABS that have just molted, so the shell is still soft and pliable. Although a crab molts many times in its life, the new shell remains soft only for a few days. It is therefore a true seasonal product. A good fishmonger who sells soft-shell crabs will nearly always clean them for you. As is true for all shellfish, however, it is important to cook them as quickly as possible once they have been killed.

The traditional Venetian method of preparing soft-shell crabs is the inspiration for this recipe. The crabs are left to sit in beaten egg until they have absorbed it. They are then dredged in flour and deep-fried in olive oil. The result is that when cooked, each crab seems to have a little frittata stuffed inside it.

8 LARGE EGGS

4 SOFT-SHELL CRABS, CLEANED (SEE NOTE)

6 RIPE ROMA TOMATOES, PEELED, SEEDED, AND FINELY CHOPPED

4 FRESH BASIL LEAVES, FINELY CHOPPED

EXTRA-VIRGIN OLIVE OIL TO TASTE

JUICE OF 1 LEMON

KOSHER SALT AND FRESHLY GROUND BLACK PEPPER TO TASTE

ABOUT 1½ CUPS FLOUR FOR DREDGING

OLIVE OIL FOR DEEP-FRYING

PESTO MAYONNAISE (SEE PAGE 227), GARLIC MAYONNAISE (SEE PAGE 227), OR OTHER MAYONNAISE OF YOUR CHOICE

BREAD OR ROLLS OF YOUR CHOICE

1 BUNCH WATERCRESS, TOUGH STEMS REMOVED, WASHED, AND DRIED

Beat the eggs in a large shallow bowl. Place the crabs in the bowl, refrigerate, and let them absorb the beaten egg for 2 to 3 hours.

In the meantime, prepare the raw tomato topping: In a small bowl, mix together the tomatoes, basil, olive oil, lemon juice, and salt and pepper to taste. Set aside at room temperature to marinate.

Season the flour with salt and pepper and place in a shallow pan for dredging. Heat the oil to 375°F in a large heavy saucepan or deep fryer.

Lift the crabs out of the egg and dredge them in the seasoned flour. Gently drop them into the hot oil and cook until they are a crunchy golden brown, 3 to 5 minutes. Lift the crabs out of the hot oil with tongs or a slotted spoon. Lay on paper towels to drain.

To assemble the panini, spread the mayonnaise of your choice on half the bread or the bottom of each roll and lay the crabs on top. Top each crab with a healthy spoonful of tomato sauce, a few sprigs of watercress, and the remaining bread or the roll tops. Cut in half and serve. Note: To clean a soft-shell crab yourself, place the live crab on a cutting board and make a quick and decisive clean cut just behind the face. Lift up the pointed ends of the soft top shell and remove the spongy gills. Turn the crab over and remove the pointed apron on its belly.

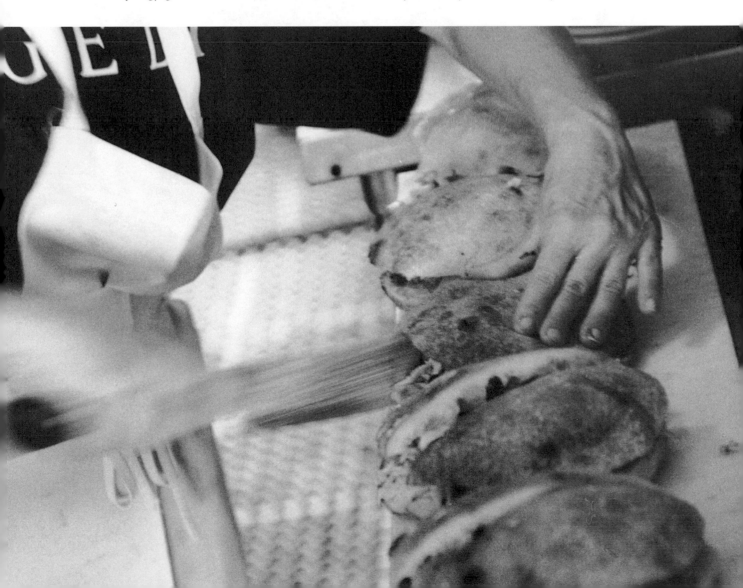

cicchetti

Venice is a strangely beautiful city. The very nature of its popularity as a unique tourist destination makes it more difficult for the casual traveler to enter and discover its secrets than in any other Italian city. Venetians protect their sanity by keeping somewhat distant from the hordes of visitors eager to taste a bit of its Byzantine elegance. Perhaps the reason I love the *bacari*, or wine bars, so much is that they present a face of Venice that is earthy and real while at the same time being fairly accessible to the tourist with a bit of curiosity. The simple signs pointing to *cicchetti e vin bon* signify that you can grab a quick bite with some history. The oldest Venetian wine bars developed as a way for the workingman to shoot back a few tiny glasses of great white wine, and quickly gulp down two or three small rolls stuffed with a satisfying savory filling, before returning to the endless, brutal labor required to keep the city afloat.

Cicchetti are a form of miniature Venetian antipasti and snack foods made to be eaten standing up at a bar. Just big enough for three or four bites, they are usually made on small rolls, some with a hard crust, some soft and shiny. They are frequently filled with a highly flavored mixture of imaginatively juxtaposed ingredients that would be overly assertive in a full-sized sandwich.

Cicchetti are really miniature panini. The variety of fillings is limited only by the cook's imagination, but there are certain expectations. The filling should pair with a glass of wine. Because cicchetti are very small, their flavors tend to be distinct and the combinations baroque. I've seen cicchetti served on the hard hollow crusty roll called a *michette* or on a soft bun made of milk dough, the top a shiny dark brown. They are nearly always presented on rolls rather than sliced bread. We often do casual luncheon parties with a buffet laden with an enormous assortment of these little beauties.

Cicchetti con gli Asparagi

ASPARAGUS, EGGS, PARMESAN

Makes 4 cicchetti

BASED ON *ASPARAGI ALLA MILANESE*, a beautiful luncheon dish of barely cooked asparagus topped with a luscious poached egg and a generous dusting of the finest grated Parmesan, these rich little mouthfuls are wonderful for a cocktail party that is pretending to be dinner.

4 SMALL SOFT ROLLS

SOFT UNSALTED BUTTER FOR SPREADING

24 THIN ASPARAGUS STALKS, TRIMMED TO 6 INCHES

4 TABLESPOONS UNSALTED BUTTER, OR MORE IF DESIRED

4 LARGE EGGS

4 OUNCES ITALIAN PARMESAN CHEESE, SHAVED OR GRATED

KOSHER SALT AND FRESHLY GROUND BLACK PEPPER TO TASTE

Slice the rolls in half. Spread them with softened butter and set aside.

Blanch the asparagus for 10 seconds in a pot of boiling salted water. Drain and immediately refresh in a bowl of ice water. When the asparagus are cold to the touch, remove from the water and lay on a kitchen towel to drain.

To fry the eggs, heat the 4 tablespoons butter in a nonstick skillet over medium heat. When the butter is hot and frothy, carefully break each egg into the pan. Sprinkle with the cheese and salt and pepper to taste. Turn the heat down and cover the pan so that the eggs baste. Cook until the eggs reach the degree of doneness you prefer.

Meanwhile, toast the rolls in a toaster oven or under a broiler until golden brown.

As the eggs finish cooking, remove them to the waiting toasted rolls. Place the asparagus in the skillet and toss them around in the remaining butter (adding more if desired) until they are heated through. Divide the asparagus among the rolls, placing them so that a bit of the tips will peek out from the sandwiches, cover with the tops of the rolls, and serve immediately.

Cicchetti all'Elizabetta

MASHED POTATOES, SALAMI, PARMESAN

Makes 6 cicchetti

POTATO CROQUETTES, A SIMPLE STREET FOOD popular in southern Italy, have been on the menu at Angeli since opening day. At the restaurant we tuck a bit of smoked mozzarella into each croquette. At the second or third bite, the melted smoky cheese mixes with the enriched potato for a positively decadent treat hidden in a humble package. Sometimes that category of restaurant dishes known as "staff food" brings forth some fortunate combinations. This variation on the extremely American mashed potato sandwich was concocted by Elisabeth Frierson, one of the original band of Angels, who stayed with us for seven years.

FOR THE POTATO CROQUETTES

2 RUSSET POTATOES, WELL SCRUBBED

KOSHER SALT TO TASTE

2 THICK SLICES SALAMI, CUT INTO SMALL DICE

1/2 CUP GRATED ITALIAN PARMESAN CHEESE

2 TABLESPOONS CHOPPED FRESH ITALIAN PARSLEY (OPTIONAL)

FRESHLY GROUND BLACK PEPPER TO TASTE

1 OUNCE SMOKED MOZZARELLA CHEESE, DICED

2 LARGE EGGS, BEATEN

1 CUP DRY BREAD CRUMBS

OLIVE OIL FOR DEEP FRYING

6 SMALL ROLLS

Place the potatoes, whole and unpeeled, in a saucepan, cover with water, and add salt to taste. Bring to a boil and cook at a slow boil until the potatoes are tender when pierced with a fork. Drain the potatoes, return to the saucepan, and toss over high heat for a few seconds to dry them out. Remove from the saucepan and let sit until cool enough to handle.

Peel the potatoes and put them through a potato ricer or food mill fitted with the coarse blade. Place into a medium bowl. Add the salami, Parmesan cheese, and parsley, if desired, and stir thoroughly with a wooden spoon. Be careful not to overmix, or the potatoes will turn gummy.

(Never use a food processor for making these potatoes!) Add salt if necessary and a generous grind of fresh pepper.

Divide the potato mixture into 6 portions. Shape each one into a log about 3 inches long and 1 inch in diameter, tucking a bit of smoked mozzarella into the center of each croquette. Place the croquettes on a platter or baking pan. Place the beaten eggs and bread crumbs in two separate small bowls. Just before frying the croquettes, dip them first in the egg, then in the bread crumbs. Meanwhile, heat the oil in a heavy saucepan or deep fryer to 375°F. (It should be hot but not smoky: Make a small croquette as a tester and gently place it in the oil.) Carefully add the croquettes, two or three at a time, to the oil and fry, gently turning them so that they brown evenly on all sides, until a deep golden brown. Remove them with a slotted spoon and place on paper towels to drain.

Cut the rolls in half and scoop out some of the inside from the bottom half of the roll. Tuck a steaming-hot croquette into each roll. Cover with the other half of the roll and serve immediately.

Cicchetti al Gorgonzola e Pera

GORGONZOLA, MASCARPONE, ONION, PEARS

Makes 4 cicchetti

THESE TOASTY ROLLS ARE BURSTING with the richness of mascarpone and the creamy bite of Gorgonzola. The tender sweetness of the caramelized pears and onions makes these a luscious snack. Serve with a soft red wine.

> ½ CUP WALNUT HALVES
>
> 4 OUNCES DOLCELATTE GORGONZOLA CHEESE
>
> 8 OUNCES MASCARPONE CHEESE
>
> 4 TABLESPOONS UNSALTED BUTTER
>
> ½ ONION, PEELED AND THINLY SLICED
>
> 2 PEARS, PEELED, CORED, AND EACH CUT LENGTHWISE INTO 8 SLICES
>
> 1 TABLESPOON SUGAR
>
> 4 CRUSTY ROLLS
>
> WALNUT OIL FOR DRIZZLING (OPTIONAL)

Preheat the oven to 400°F. Put the walnuts on a baking sheet and toast them in the oven for about 7 minutes, or until golden brown. Set aside to cool, then coarsely chop.

In a small bowl, beat together the Gorgonzola and mascarpone cheeses with a wooden spoon. When they are well mixed, add the chopped walnuts and stir to distribute them evenly throughout the cheese.

Heat the butter in a medium skillet until melted and frothy. Add the onion and cook until it begins to soften and turn golden. Add the pears and sugar and continue cooking until the onions and pears are slightly caramelized, about 15 minutes. The pears should be tender yet still retain their shape.

Meanwhile, slice the rolls in half. Toast in a toaster oven or under a broiler until golden brown.

Generously slather the bottom half of the rolls with the cheese-walnut mixture. Top with the warm pear-onion mixture. Drizzle the top half of the rolls with a bit of walnut oil, if desired, and place atop the filling. Serve immediately.

Cicchetti d'Ivan

FRESH TUNA, WHITE BEANS, CELERY

Makes 6 cicchetti

MY FRIEND/"ADOPTED BROTHER" IVAN THILLET worked with me as my pasta chef a million years ago when I was the head chef at Verdi Ristorante di Musica in Santa Monica. He was—and continues to be—famous for his eccentric brand of staff meals, made from combinations of the food ready on "the cooking line." This delicious little bite was inspired by his pairing of grilled tuna with pasta e fagioli soup and bread. *Insalata di tonno con fagioli* is a traditional Italian antipasto found in nearly every region.

2 TUNA STEAKS, ½ INCH THICK (OR 2 LARGE CANS TUNA PACKED IN SPRING WATER OR OLIVE OIL)

EXTRA-VIRGIN OLIVE OIL

KOSHER SALT AND FRESHLY GROUND BLACK PEPPER TO TASTE

1 LEMON

1 CUP COOKED CANNELLINI OR GREAT NORTHERN BEANS

1 CELERY STALK WITH LEAVES, TRIMMED, WASHED, AND THINLY SLICED

¼ SMALL RED ONION, PEELED AND THINLY SLICED

6 SMALL ROLLS

To cook the fish, heat a charcoal or gas grill or ridged stovetop griddle until very hot, or preheat the broiler. Lightly rub the grill with an oiled towel to prevent the fish from sticking. Brush each steak with a bit of oil and sprinkle with salt and pepper to taste. Place the fish steaks on the grill or under the broiler and cook for approximately 3 minutes per side, or until the fish feels firm when pressed with your finger.

Place the tuna in a mixing bowl. Using a fork, break the tuna apart into rough pieces about ½ inch in size. (If you are using canned tuna, drain it and place it in a bowl.) Using a citrus zester, zest the lemon directly into the bowl of tuna. Cut the zested lemon in half and squeeze the juice over the fish. Add the beans, celery, onion, and oil to taste. Toss very gently to avoid mashing the beans. Adjust the seasoning with salt and pepper if necessary.

Slice the rolls in half. Spoon the mixture in the bottom half and place the top half atop the filling. Serve immediately.

Cicchetti di Tonno e Carciofi

TUNA, ARTICHOKE HEARTS, OLIVES

Makes 4 cicchetti

TUNA AND ARTICHOKE HEARTS ARE A serendipitous combination. The acidic spiciness of the marinated hearts cuts the fishiness of the tuna and adds a bit of richness without resorting to mayonnaise. These little treats can be filled and set aside in the refrigerator up to two hours ahead.

4 CRUSTY DINNER ROLLS

ONE 6-OUNCE CAN TUNA IN SPRING WATER, DRAINED

½ RED BELL PEPPER, STEM, SEEDS, AND TOUGH WHITE RIBS REMOVED

ONE 6-OUNCE JAR MARINATED ARTICHOKE HEARTS, DRAINED AND HALVED LENGTHWISE

12 KALAMATA OLIVES, PITTED AND QUARTERED LENGTHWISE

4 VERY THIN SLICES RED ONION, MINCED

SMALL HANDFUL OF COARSELY CHOPPED FRESH ITALIAN PARSLEY

1 LEMON

EXTRA-VIRGIN OLIVE OIL TO TASTE

FRESHLY GROUND BLACK PEPPER TO TASTE

Cut the tops off the rolls and set aside. Remove some of the inside from each roll to create a nice hollow space to fill up with the tuna mixture. Discard half this bread and coarsely chop the rest. Cover the rolls with plastic wrap and set aside.

Place the tuna in a medium bowl and flake the meat apart with a fork. Add the reserved chopped bread. Cut the pepper into very thin strips; if the pepper is very long, cut the strips crosswise in half. Add the pepper strips to the tuna with the artichokes, olives, onion, and parsley. Using a citrus zester, zest the lemon directly into the bowl of tuna. Cut the zested lemon in half and squeeze the juice into the tuna mixture. Add olive oil and pepper to taste. Let sit for at least 1 hour, covered, in the refrigerator, to marry the flavors.

Spoon the tuna mixture into the rolls. Replace the tops and serve.

Cicchetti al Granseola

POTATO, CRABMEAT, FENNEL, HERBS

Makes 6 cicchetti

OUR MOST POPULAR MEAL FOR CATERING is the cocktail buffet. There is enough food to satisfy even the hungriest grazer, with so much variety to keep the appetite interested for hours. We often tuck these special little rolls filled with the unusual combination of crabmeat, potato, and fennel into a linen-lined basket on the buffet.

1 LARGE RED POTATO, PEELED

1/2 POUND CRABMEAT, PREFERABLY DUNGENESS OR BLUE CRAB

1 STALK CELERY, MINCED

1 SMALL FENNEL BULB, TOUGH OUTER LAYERS REMOVED, CORED, AND MINCED

SMALL HANDFUL OF COARSELY CHOPPED ITALIAN PARSLEY

5 FRESH BASIL LEAVES, FINELY CHOPPED

1 GARLIC CLOVE, PEELED

JUICE OF 1 LEMON

EXTRA-VIRGIN OLIVE OIL TO TASTE

KOSHER SALT AND FRESHLY GROUND BLACK PEPPER TO TASTE

6 SMALL ROLLS

Place the potato in a saucepan of salted cold water to cover and bring to a boil over high heat. Lower the heat to a gentle boil and cook until the potato is tender when pierced with the tip of a knife. Drain and let cool. When the potato is cool enough to handle, cut it into small dice.

Put the crabmeat in a mixing bowl and pick through it to make sure that it is free of shell. Add the potato, celery, fennel, parsley, and basil and stir gently to mix. Put the garlic through a press directly into the bowl of crabmeat. Add the lemon juice and olive oil to taste. Season with salt and pepper to taste. Cover with plastic wrap and refrigerate for at least 1 hour to allow the flavors to come together.

To assemble the cicchetti, slice the rolls in half. Remove a bit of the inside from the bottom halves and tuck some crabmeat filling into each. Top with the remaining roll halves and serve.

bruschetta

My most fantastic memory of bruschetta is sitting with a small group of very good friends around a perfectly banked fire one night at the very beginning of autumn. The first chill is in the air. The fire sits in a ring of stones, surrounded by all of us gathered together under the stars. We have cut big chunky slices of bread from an enormous wood-fired loaf and threaded them onto sturdy twigs from nearby trees. As we carefully toast our bread over the fire, we sit amiably chatting, letting contented silences be part of the conversation. An occasional slurp of smooth red wine from a friend's vines intermingles with the words. When each piece of bread has been toasted to its owner's idea of perfection, "ouches" and grunts replace the conversation as the hot toasts are quickly plucked off the sticks to be rubbed with garlic cloves. Then comes the almost ritual anointing of oil: strong and spicy, fruity, thick *olio nuovo* not yet five hours from the press. Silence again as we eat, leaning over as the oil drips off happy faces to be licked off chilled fingers.

How could you duplicate such an experience at a caffè on Melrose? You don't even try. You simply present the best ingredients with the most warmth possible to encourage the possibility that others will create for themselves rich moments out of simplicity.

In its simplest form, bruschetta is grilled bread rubbed with garlic and drizzled with extra-virgin olive oil, but it can be enriched with a variety of ingredients to add a whole new meaning to the term *open-faced*. To make good bruschetta, you must have a bread that is firm of crumb and has a hard crust. A top-quality estate-bottled extra-virgin olive oil is also essential. Pick one that has a flavor you enjoy, whether peppery and strong from Tuscany or Umbria, light and fruity from Liguria, or golden and grassy from Sicily and the Abruzzi. Eating bruschetta is the perfect way to try different oils. Get acquainted with extra-virgins from France, Spain, and Greece as well.

The most romantic way to grill the bread is over an open fire or in the fireplace. However, for everyday satisfaction, a charcoal or gas grill, broiler, toaster oven, or toaster works perfectly well.

Bruschetta Aglio e Olio

GARLIC, OIL

Makes 4 bruschetta

THE CLASSIC ITALIAN GARLIC BREAD, from which all other more baroque combinations come. I prefer the slices cut about three quarters of an inch thick so that your teeth get the satisfaction of biting through a crusty top layer and into a softer layer of crumb. If you cut the slices thin, after toasting they will be too crispy and each bite will result in broken toast and crumbs everywhere.

4 SLICES BREAD FOR BRUSCHETTA
2 GARLIC CLOVES, PEELED
EXTRA-VIRGIN OLIVE OIL FOR DRIZZLING
KOSHER SALT AND FRESHLY GROUND BLACK PEPPER TO TASTE

Grill or toast the bread so that the surface is a light golden brown and the inside is still a bit soft.

When the bread is properly toasted, lightly rub the peeled garlic cloves over it. Place the bruschetta on a serving plate and drizzle olive oil to taste over it. Sprinkle with salt and pepper as desired. Serve immediately.

Bruschetta al Pomodoro e Rucola

TOMATO, ARUGULA

Makes 4 large bruschetta

AT ANGELI WE TRY TO VARY THE SELECTION of our bruschetta from week to week so our customers may try different toppings. But day in and out, the most requested is this recipe, at its best during summer months when tomatoes are luscious and juicy.

3 LARGE RIPE ROUND TOMATOES, STEM ENDS REMOVED AND DICED

2 SMALL BUNCHES ARUGULA, TOUGH STEMS REMOVED, WELL WASHED, DRIED, AND COARSELY CHOPPED

EXTRA-VIRGIN OLIVE OIL TO TASTE

KOSHER SALT AND FRESHLY GROUND BLACK PEPPER TO TASTE

4 SLICES BREAD FOR BRUSCHETTA

2 GARLIC CLOVES, PEELED

Place the tomatoes and arugula in a small bowl. Add olive oil and salt and pepper to taste and gently mix together until the juices of the tomato mix with the olive oil.

Grill or toast the bread so that the surface is a light golden brown yet the inside is still a bit soft.

When the bruschetta is properly toasted, lightly rub the peeled garlic cloves over the bread. Spoon the tomato-arugula mixture onto the bruschetta. Serve with lots of napkins.

Bruschetta alla Ricotta e Peperoni

HERBED RICOTTA, SWEET RED PEPPERS, OLIVES, CAPERS

Makes 6 bruschetta

A SIMPLE LIGHT OPEN-FACED SANDWICH with the savory addition of sautéed roasted peppers and olives, this is a favorite with our vegetarian crowd. The trick is to use the freshest ricotta you can find. At Angeli we are incredibly lucky to have available the products of Italian artisan cheesemakers who operate locally. Virgilio, the entrepreneur who started Italcheese, was the first to achieve success making Italian-style fresh *fior di latte* (literally, "flower of the milk") cheese in Southern California. We used his product for many years.

Recently I met Vito from the small town of Gioia del Colle in Puglia. He started a fresh cheese company in Los Angeles called Caseificio Gioia and is still small enough to produce a cheese most closely approximating in taste and texture the product of regional Italian cheesemakers. I had visited Gioia del Colle just three weeks before he stopped at our door—it was too amazing a coincidence to ignore. When I discovered that I had toured his uncle's cheese factory in Gioia, I knew it was the angels at work again!

1 POUND FRESH RICOTTA CHEESE

1/4 CUP FINELY CHOPPED FRESH ITALIAN PARSLEY

6 LARGE FRESH BASIL LEAVES, CUT INTO FINE JULIENNE

JUICE OF 1 LEMON

EXTRA-VIRGIN OLIVE OIL

2 GARLIC CLOVES, PEELED AND THINLY SLICED

ONE 16-OUNCE JAR ROASTED RED PEPPERS, RINSED, SEEDED, AND CUT LENGTHWISE INTO THIN STRIPS

1/4 CUP PITTED KALAMATA OR OTHER OIL-CURED OLIVES

1 TEASPOON CAPERS

KOSHER SALT AND FRESHLY GROUND BLACK PEPPER TO TASTE

6 THICK SLICES BREAD FOR BRUSCHETTA

1 GARLIC CLOVE, PEELED

In a small bowl, mix together the ricotta, herbs, lemon juice, and olive oil to taste. Set aside to allow the flavors to marry while you prepare the peppers. (This mixture can sit in the refrigerator for as long as 2 days before using.)

Heat just enough olive oil to barely cover the bottom of a small skillet. Add the garlic and cook over low heat until it starts to turn golden. Immediately add the peppers, olives, and capers to the skillet. Sauté briefly over medium heat, just until the mixture is hot and the flavors have blended. Add salt if necessary and pepper to taste. Remove from the heat and spoon the mixture, with all the cooking juices, into a bowl to cool slightly, or cool to room temperature.

Grill or lightly toast the bread. Rub the bread with the garlic clove and drizzle on a bit of olive oil. Slather the ricotta mixture over the bruschetta. Top with a spoonful of the warm or room-temperature peppers, being sure to include a bit of the flavorful cooking juices. Arrange on a large platter and serve immediately.

Bruschetta con Scamorza e Pomodori

FRESH TOMATO, OREGANO, SMOKED MOZZARELLA

Makes 4 large bruschetta

I HAD MY FIRST PLATE OF GRILLED SMOKED MOZZARELLA topped with this tomato mixture at La Latteria in Milan in 1982, and when Angeli Caffè opened, it quickly became one of our most popular starters. It was a simple evolutionary step to move the cheese from a plate onto a piece of good bread with a firm crumb.

3 RIPE YET FIRM ROMA TOMATOES, STEM ENDS REMOVED AND CUT INTO SMALL DICE

PINCH OF DRIED OREGANO

KOSHER SALT AND FRESHLY GROUND BLACK PEPPER TO TASTE

EXTRA-VIRGIN OLIVE OIL TO TASTE

4 THICK SLICES BREAD FOR BRUSCHETTA

FOUR $1/4$-INCH-THICK SLICES SMOKED MOZZARELLA

In a small bowl, mix together the chopped tomatoes, oregano, salt and pepper, and olive oil to taste. Set aside while you broil the bread and cheese. Preheat the broiler. Top each slice of bread with a slice of cheese. Broil about 6 inches from the heat until the cheese is bubbly and golden brown in spots. Remove from the heat, place on a serving platter, and top each slice with a generous spoonful of the seasoned tomatoes with their juices. Serve with plenty of napkins.

Bruschetta ai Funghi

MUSHROOMS, HERBS, PROSCIUTTO, FONTINA

Makes 4 large bruschetta

TRUE ITALIAN FONTINA IS A SWEET, nutty-tasting cheese that melts more smoothly than nearly any other cheese. It pairs perfectly with prosciutto and mushrooms. Cremini mushrooms are beginning to pop up at specialty produce markets all over the country. These are the brown domestic mushrooms of my youth before the "white" mushroom was introduced and pushed them out of the marketplace in the 1960s. If you can find cremini, use them. They have more depth of flavor than the ubiquitous white mushroom.

2 TO 4 TABLESPOONS UNSALTED BUTTER

2 GARLIC CLOVES, PEELED, 1 MINCED AND 1 LEFT WHOLE

16 CREMINI OR WHITE MUSHROOMS, STEMS TRIMMED, WIPED CLEAN, AND CUT INTO THICK SLICES

1 SPRIG THYME

KOSHER SALT AND FRESHLY GROUND BLACK PEPPER TO TASTE

4 THICK SLICES BREAD FOR BRUSCHETTA

2 THIN SLICES PROSCIUTTO, CUT IN HALF LENGTHWISE

4 THIN SLICES ITALIAN FONTINA CHEESE

Heat the butter in a skillet over high heat until it is frothy. Add the minced garlic clove, the mushrooms, thyme, and salt and pepper to taste. Cook over high heat, stirring frequently, until the mushrooms are golden and crusty. Remove the thyme sprig and discard. Set the mushrooms aside.

Preheat the broiler. Toast the bread just until barely golden.

Rub the bread with the remaining garlic clove. Top each slice of bread with a piece of prosciutto and a slice of Fontina. Place on the broiler tray and broil until the cheese melts and is bubbly with a few golden dots. Remove the bruschetta to a serving plate. Place a couple of tablespoonfuls of the cooked mushrooms atop each. Serve immediately.

tramezzini

Tramezzini are the Italians' fantasy of English tea sandwiches. They often consist of a frugal amount of filling, often smooth and rich, set between thin slices of bread. (Shocking to report, it is usually mass-produced *pan carre*, ordinary white sandwich bread.) They are a snack meant to be bolted down in a few quick easily digested bites and can be found at any bar in Italy, arrayed in a shallow glass display case covered with white cloth napkins. Of course, there are exceptions, such as the elegant bar down the way from Caffè Greco in Rome, where Roman high society gathers for tramezzini tartufati, with white or black truffles—or maybe porcini—during the season.

We sometimes serve tramezzini at Italian-style "high teas," but more frequently they make their appearance as cocktail party canapés, cut into triangles, circles, or squares. I have never had any use for hors d'oeuvres that are basically bread with an insipid filling, so it took us a while to develop highly flavorful offerings that satisfied me. They all can be spread smoothly and thinly enough on a good soft bread or a very thinly sliced sturdy loaf. However, many of them work equally well atop crostini or piped into tiny pastry boats.

When you are preparing the fillings for tramezzini or canapés, be sure to buy a good bakery loaf and have it sliced very thin for you. If you are making canapés for a party, keep a barely damp kitchen towel nearby to cover the finished treats as you work to prevent them from drying out.

Tramezzini di Caprino al Miele

WHITE OR EGG PULLMAN, WALNUTS

THIS FILLING WAS INSPIRED BY my days around the Iranian breakfast table with friends. The pairing of a smooth-textured yet acidic cheese with the sweet creaminess of unblended honey and the special flavor of fresh raw walnuts is a flavor that I crave from time to time. My preferred honey for this dish is either the Italian solid Acacia honey or the famous lavender honey of Provence.

GOAT CHEESE, SOFTENED

BREAD OF YOUR CHOICE, THINLY SLICED

UNBLENDED HONEY

COARSELY CHOPPED (UNTOASTED) WALNUTS, FOR GARNISH

Spread an even layer of goat cheese on half the bread. Spread a very thin layer of honey atop the cheese. Sprinkle walnuts over all. Top with the remaining bread and gently press down to firm up the tramezzini. Cut to the size and shape you desire and serve.

"Toast" di Formaggi Misti

POTATO-DILL, PUMPERNICKEL, WHITE

Serves 8 to 16

STEPPING FROM A ROARINGLY NOISY NARROW STREET into a bar for a quick *spremuta* and a *"toast"* is one of the pleasures of Italian urban life. No bar would be complete without the double-sided ridged griddle used to cook these simple sandwiches of cheese and prosciutto. We take the idea one step farther to create an especially savory bite by using a mixture of some of the greatest hits of Italian cheese. They combine the smooth acidity of goat cheese, the creamy bite of Gorgonzola dolcelatte, the rich nuttiness of Taleggio, and the light sweetness of mozzarella. We simply sauté the "toasts" in butter, but you can use the griddle side of a waffle iron for a more traditional "toast."

2 OUNCES FRESH GOAT CHEESE

2 OUNCES DOLCELATTE GORGONZOLA CHEESE

2 OUNCES TALEGGIO CHEESE

2 OUNCES MOZZARELLA CHEESE

DIJON MUSTARD

8 THIN SLICES BREAD OF YOUR CHOICE

4 TABLESPOONS UNSALTED BUTTER

In a small bowl, beat all the cheeses together with a wooden spoon. Spread a bit of mustard over half the slices of bread. Spread the cheese mixture over the mustard, leaving a ½-inch border free so that there is room for the cheese to ooze outward. Place the remaining bread slices on top and press down firmly.

Melt the butter in a large skillet and toast the tramezzini until golden on both sides. Remove from the heat and let stand for a minute so the cheese isn't completely runny. Cut diagonally into quarters and serve immediately.

Tramezzini di Prosciutto e Mozzarella

WHITE, FOCACCIA

CALLED PANINO SEMPLICE, "THE SIMPLE SANDWICH," at Angeli, this is one of my favorites and it is the panino most frequently ordered by Italians visiting Los Angeles. I suppose that is because it incorporates three nearly primal Italian foods, great bread, sweet prosciutto, and fresh, milky mozzarella. We serve it on Pane degli Angeli (page 95) in the restaurant, which really makes it qualify as a full-fledged panino, but it is also one of our most requested tramezzini for parties.

Drizzle a little olive oil on the bread for extra flavor and richness if you want, but the tramezzino is equally good with absolutely no condiments at all. The key to making the simple ingredients work is to use prosciutto di Parma, sliced very thin, and to put just a couple of slices in the sandwich. The prosciutto should really act as a condiment for the mozzarella.

PROSCIUTTO DI PARMA, THINLY SLICED

FRESH MOZZARELLA CHEESE, DRAINED AND THINLY SLICED

BREAD OF YOUR CHOICE, THINLY SLICED

Place the prosciutto and mozzarella on half the slices of bread and top with the remaining bread. Cut to the size and shape you desire and serve.

Tramezzini di Bresaola e Mascarpone

PUMPERNICKEL, WHITE

Serves 8 to 16

THE TRADITIONAL NORTHERN ITALIAN ANTIPASTO COMBINATION of bresaola—air-cured beef—mascarpone, and arugula is enriched in these elegant tea sandwiches with pine nuts and a bit of truffle oil.

8 THIN SLICES BREAD OF YOUR CHOICE

4 OUNCES MASCARPONE CHEESE

PINE NUTS

8 VERY THIN SLICES BRESAOLA

1 SMALL BUNCH ARUGULA, TOUGH STEMS REMOVED, WELL WASHED, AND DRIED

1 LEMON, HALVED

TRUFFLE OIL (OPTIONAL)

Spread half the bread slices with the mascarpone. Sprinkle a few pine nuts over the cheese, then top with the bresaola. Garnish each with a few leaves of arugula and a light drizzle of lemon juice and truffle oil, if you desire. Cut to the size and shape you desire and serve.

Tramezzini ai Gamberi

WHITE, EGG, PUMPERNICKEL, POTATO-DILL

Serves 6 to 12

WE LOVE THIS FILLING! EQUALLY GOOD in tramezzini or atop crostini, it combines nearly everyone's favorite tastes. The rich orangy-pink color of the filling makes it particularly suitable for serving open-faced. This unusual puree of shrimp, butter, tomato, basil, and watercress is also well suited to be piped into cucumber boats.

4 TABLESPOONS UNSALTED BUTTER, SOFTENED

2 TEASPOONS TOMATO PASTE

1/2 TEASPOON SUGAR

3 FRESH BASIL LEAVES, FINELY CHOPPED

FRESHLY GROUND BLACK PEPPER TO TASTE

1/4 POUND COOKED PEELED SHRIMP, MINCED

6 THIN SLICES BREAD OF YOUR CHOICE

1/2 SMALL BUNCH WATERCRESS, COARSE STEMS REMOVED, WASHED, AND DRIED

In a medium bowl, beat the butter with a whisk or wooden spoon, or an electric mixer, until it is light and fluffy. Add the tomato paste, sugar, basil, and pepper and beat vigorously to mix. Stir in the shrimp. (To make the puree in the food processor, simply combine the butter, tomato paste, sugar, basil, and pepper and process with the steel blade until smooth. Add the shrimp and pulse to blend.)

To assemble the tramezzini, generously spread the shrimp butter onto the sliced bread. Garnish with watercress sprigs. Serve open-faced, cut to the size and shape you wish.

Tramezzini del Te

WHITE, EGG, PUMPERNICKEL, POTATO-DILL

THIS TRADITIONAL COMBINATION is wonderfully comforting served on thinly sliced egg bread.

OLIVE MAYONNAISE (SEE PAGE 227)

BREAD OF YOUR CHOICE, THINLY SLICED

HARD-COOKED EGGS, SLICED

HOTHOUSE CUCUMBER, PEELED AND CUT INTO THIN ROUNDS

KOSHER SALT TO TASTE

CHOPPED FRESH CHIVES

Spread olive mayonnaise on all the slices of bread. Layer the sliced eggs and cucumber on half the bread. Sprinkle with salt to taste and chives. Place the remaining bread atop the filling and gently press down to firm the tramezzini. Cut to the size and shape you desire.

Nearly every cook has a repertoire of essential recipes that are used over and over and represent an oft-used flavor palette. Sometimes these essentials, such as the tomato sauces, appear center stage; others are hits of flavor that when added to a familiar recipe easily and quickly make it something special. Others are really just simple techniques—steaming open shellfish or roasting and peeling peppers—that restaurant chefs use all the time, but cooking at home is more relaxed and enjoyable with the addition of these techniques to the mix. At Angeli, as in most good restaurants, we have our own "secret" dishes that are, in fact, essential to the *cucina* we serve every day. We are happy to share them with you.

...ked Tomato Sauce for Pizza

...nough for six 8-inch pizzas

...K FOR THE SWEETEST VINE-RIPENED canned tomatoes you can find. Taste them raw out of the can and if you find them a bit too acidic, add a pinch of sugar to the sauce. This sauce freezes beautifully for up to one month and keeps covered in the refrigerator for up to three days.

ONE 28-OUNCE CAN ITALIAN OR ITALIAN-STYLE CRUSHED TOMATOES, DRAINED
2 TABLESPOONS OLIVE OIL
KOSHER SALT AND FRESHLY GROUND BLACK PEPPER TO TASTE

Put the tomatoes, olive oil, and salt and pepper into the bowl of a food processor fitted with the steel blade, and blend for 1 minute. Or pass the ingredients through the medium disk of a food mill.

Tomato-Basil Sauce

Makes 2 cups

A FOOD MILL IS MY ONE indispensable piece of kitchen equipment. Nothing is better for making a delicious fresh tomato sauce quickly and with little mess or trouble. The advantage is that the tomatoes can be cooked with their skin and seeds. When the sauce is thick enough, simply pass it through the medium or coarse disk. No more peeling, seeding, and chopping tomatoes!

1/4 CUP EXTRA-VIRGIN OLIVE OIL

2 GARLIC CLOVES, PEELED AND MINCED

12 ROMA TOMATOES, STEM ENDS REMOVED AND CUT INTO QUARTERS, OR ONE 28-OUNCE CAN ITALIAN OR ITALIAN-STYLE PEAR TOMATOES IN JUICE

8 LARGE FRESH BASIL LEAVES

KOSHER SALT AND FRESHLY GROUND BLACK PEPPER TO TASTE

Heat the oil in a large skillet over medium heat. Add the garlic and sauté just until the garlic gives off its characteristic aroma. Add the tomatoes and cook over medium-high heat, stirring frequently until the tomatoes begin to break down and form a sauce. Add the basil, season with salt and pepper, and continue cooking, stirring occasionally, until the sauce is thick and no longer watery. Remove from the heat and put the sauce through the medium disk of a food mill. The sauce keeps for up to 3 days, covered, in the refrigerator or for up to 1 month in the freezer.

Béchamel Sauce

Makes 2 cups

I USE THIS CLASSIC WHITE SAUCE in baked recipes to add a touch of creaminess to certain dishes.

4 TABLESPOONS UNSALTED BUTTER

3 TABLESPOONS ALL-PURPOSE FLOUR

2 CUPS MILK

KOSHER SALT AND FRESHLY GROUND BLACK PEPPER TO TASTE

Melt the butter in a small saucepan over low heat. Add the flour and stir to form a smooth paste. Heat the milk in a separate saucepan. When it is hot but not boiling, pour it into the roux (the butter-flour mixture), stirring constantly with a whisk or wooden spoon. Cook over low heat, stirring, until the sauce thickens and the floury taste is gone. Add salt and pepper to taste.

Red Onion Condiment

Makes 1½ cups

A SIMPLE, SHARP-FLAVORED ADDITION TO many panini.

1 SMALL RED ONION, PEELED

¼ CUP EXTRA-VIRGIN OLIVE OIL

2 TABLESPOONS RED WINE VINEGAR

1 TEASPOON DRIED OREGANO

KOSHER SALT AND FRESHLY GROUND BLACK PEPPER TO TASTE

Slice the onion as thinly as possible: The easiest and safest way to do this is first to cut the onion in half lengthwise. Lay one half cut side down on a cutting board and use a sharp knife to thinly slice the onion crosswise. Repeat with the other half. Place the sliced onion in a bowl. Add the olive oil, vinegar, oregano, and salt and pepper to taste and mix well. Cover and store in the refrigerator. This keeps approximately 1 week.

Roasted Pepper–Olive Condiment

Makes 2½ cups

THIS SIMPLE-TO-MAKE CONDIMENT IS packed with flavor. It is delicious atop pizze or bruschetta, tucked into panini, or tossed into hot pasta.

OLIVE OIL

2 GARLIC CLOVES, PEELED AND THINLY SLICED

One 16-OUNCE JAR ROASTED PEPPERS, RINSED, SEEDED, AND CUT LENGTHWISE INTO STRIPS

¼ CUP PITTED KALAMATA OLIVES

1 TEASPOON CAPERS, RINSED

KOSHER SALT AND FRESHLY GROUND PEPPER TO TASTE

Heat just enough olive oil to barely cover the bottom of a small skillet. Add the garlic and cook slowly over low heat until it starts to turn golden. Immediately add the peppers, olives, and capers to the skillet. Sauté briefly over medium heat just until the mixture is hot and the flavors have mixed together. Add salt if necessary and pepper to taste. Spoon the mixture with all the cooking juices into a bowl to cool. This keeps, covered, in the refrigerator for up to 3 days.

Garlic-Parmesan Dressing

Makes 1½ cups

THE NOW-FAMOUS ANGELI DRESSING IS actually one I grew up with, watching my Aunt Ruth and my mom make it nearly every day of my childhood. The secret is a good aged red wine vinegar. It is the slightly mellowed sharpness playing off the hot garlic and rich cheese that gives the dressing its character.

2 GARLIC CLOVES, PEELED

1 TEASPOON KOSHER SALT

1 CUP EXTRA-VIRGIN OLIVE OIL

⅓ CUP RED WINE VINEGAR, OR MORE TO TASTE

¼ CUP GRATED ITALIAN PARMESAN CHEESE

FRESHLY GROUND BLACK PEPPER TO TASTE

Push the garlic through a garlic press into a small bowl. Sprinkle the salt over the pressed garlic. Using the back of a wooden spoon press and mash the salt into the garlic. Add the olive oil to the garlic-salt mixture. Whisk in the vinegar, Parmesan cheese, and pepper.

Sun-Dried Tomato Pesto

Makes about 1 cup

SUN-DRIED TOMATO PESTO IS AN extremely versatile condiment. Its earthy deep red color and intense sweet tomato taste give a complex jolt to many dishes. Good on pizza, bruschetta, panini, tramezzini, and pasta.

ONE 8-OUNCE JAR SUN-DRIED TOMATOES PACKED IN OIL

2 SPRIGS THYME, LEAVES ONLY (OPTIONAL)

EXTRA-VIRGIN OLIVE OIL AS NEEDED

Empty the jar of sun-dried tomatoes and its oil into the bowl of a food processor fitted with the steel blade. Add the thyme, if desired. Process to a smooth puree, adding additional extra-virgin olive oil 1 tablespoon at a time if needed to achieve the texture you desire. This pesto will keep for up to 2 weeks in the refrigerator if it is topped off with olive oil (see Basil Pesto).

Pesto alla Genovese (Basil Pesto)

Makes 2 cups

A CLASSIC BASIL PESTO FROM LIGURIA. Use it on pizze, focacce, panini, or pasta whenever you want the full flavor of summer herb gardens.

> 2 CUPS FIRMLY PACKED FRESH BASIL LEAVES
>
> 4 TO 6 GARLIC CLOVES, PEELED
>
> 1/4 CUP EXTRA-VIRGIN OLIVE OIL
>
> 1/2 CUP GRATED ITALIAN PARMESAN CHEESE
>
> KOSHER SALT AND FRESHLY GROUND BLACK PEPPER TO TASTE
>
> 1/4 CUP TOASTED PINE NUTS OR WALNUTS
>
> EXTRA-VIRGIN OLIVE OIL FOR STIRRING (OPTIONAL)

Place the basil and garlic in a food processor fitted with the steel blade. Process until finely chopped. With the machine running, add half the oil in a slow, steady stream. Add the Parmesan cheese and process until the cheese is well blended. With the machine running, slowly add the remaining oil and process until creamy. Season with salt and pepper. Add the nuts and pulse until the nuts are coarsely chopped. Use immediately, or pour into a container, and top with a thin layer of olive oil, if desired, to prevent the basil from turning dark. Tightly seal and refrigerate.

Flavored Mayonnaise

Makes approximately 1¼ cups

THOSE OF YOU WHO ARE COMFORTABLE enough with your source of eggs to eat them uncooked and who enjoy making mayonnaise probably already have a favorite recipe. However, I know that many of you are uncomfortable using raw eggs in your cooking. If this is the case, simply use the best quality store-bought mayonnaise available. It takes very little time to create a special condiment to complement your favorite panini or tramezzini fillings. Use the following proportions as a guide when creating your own variations.

THE BASIC METHOD FOR FLAVORED MAYONNAISE IS AS FOLLOWS:
Place the mayonnaise in a small bowl. Add the flavorings and stir well to mix. Cover with plastic wrap, pressing the wrap directly against the mayonnaise, and refrigerate for at least 1 hour to allow the flavors to marry. Most flavored mayonnaises will keep perfectly well for up to 1 week when properly stored.

Horseradish Mayonnaise

1 CUP HOMEMADE OR STORE-BOUGHT MAYONNAISE

1 TABLESPOON HORSERADISH

JUICE OF ½ SMALL LEMON

FRESHLY GROUND BLACK PEPPER TO TASTE

Piquant Mayonnaise

1 CUP HOMEMADE OR STORE-BOUGHT MAYONNAISE

1 TABLESPOON CAPERS, COARSELY CHOPPED

¼ CUP CHOPPED FRESH ITALIAN PARSLEY

1 SHALLOT, PEELED AND MINCED

1 GARLIC CLOVE, PEELED AND MINCED

JUICE OF ½ SMALL LEMON

FRESHLY GROUND BLACK PEPPER TO TASTE

Olive Mayonnaise

1 CUP HOMEMADE OR STORE-BOUGHT MAYONNAISE

1 TO 2 TABLESPOONS BLACK OLIVE PASTE (TO TASTE)

FRESHLY GROUND BLACK PEPPER TO TASTE

Pesto Mayonnaise

1 CUP HOMEMADE OR STORE-BOUGHT MAYONNAISE

¼ CUP BASIL PESTO (SEE PAGE 225)

FRESHLY GROUND BLACK PEPPER TO TASTE

Garlic Mayonnaise

1 CUP HOMEMADE OR STORE-BOUGHT MAYONNAISE

5 GARLIC CLOVES, PEELED AND PUT THROUGH A GARLIC PRESS

JUICE OF ½ LEMON (OPTIONAL)

FRESHLY GROUND BLACK PEPPER TO TASTE

Roasted Red Peppers

MEATY SCARLET SWEET PEPPERS are an intrinsic part of the Italian kitchen. Feel free to experiment with color and flavor with the newer varieties in yellow, orange, brown, and even black.

RED BELL PEPPERS

Roast the peppers over a gas flame or under the broiler until the skin is blackened, turning occasionally with a pair of tongs. Place the peppers in a plastic bag, seal, and let steam for 15 to 20 minutes. Remove the skins and seeds under cold running water. If you wish to make the peppers a few days ahead do so. They will keep up to four days if well wrapped in plastic.

Caramelized Garlic

USE ONLY YOUNG, FIRM, UNSPROUTED GARLIC for this condiment. Remember that the garlic will continue to cook after you remove it from the fire, so take care not to wait too long to turn off the heat. These soft, mellow, nutty-tasting cloves can be used in nearly any dish you like, from pasta to pizza to panini. The resulting garlic-infused oil is delicious atop pizza or drizzled onto a roast hot from the oven.

PEELED GARLIC CLOVES
OLIVE OIL TO COVER

Place the garlic cloves in a small deep saucepan and barely cover with olive oil. Cook over low to medium-low heat until the garlic is golden, watching constantly, as it cooks quickly. Remove from the heat when the garlic is barely golden and dotted with darker brown. Allow to cool. Store the garlic in the refrigerator, submerged in the cooking oil, for up to 2 weeks.

Garlicky Bread Crumbs

ALMOST LIKE SMALL CROUTONS, GOLDEN, garlicky crunchy crumbs add texture and flavor to any pasta dish. The "sacrificing of the bread crumbs" is an old Angeli tradition—it is so easy to let them go from not quite golden brown enough to burnt if you are not vigilant.

GOOD-QUALITY FRESH BREAD, CRUSTS REMOVED AND CUBED
MINCED GARLIC TO TASTE
KOSHER SALT AND FRESHLY GROUND BLACK PEPPER TO TASTE
EXTRA-VIRGIN OLIVE OIL AS NEEDED

Preheat the oven to 350°F.

In a food processor fitted with the steel blade, process the bread into coarse crumbs. Place the crumbs in a large mixing bowl. Toss with the garlic and salt and pepper until well mixed. Add just enough olive oil to slightly moisten the crumbs. Spread the seasoned bread crumbs on a baking sheet and bake until golden brown stirring occasionally. Watch carefully, as the crumbs can burn in a matter of seconds.

Caramelized Onions

AN EXPLOSION OF SWEET, PUNGENT FLAVOR that adds character to nearly any savory dish.

OLIVE OIL

THINLY SLICED ONIONS

$1/4$ CUP WATER PER MEDIUM ONION

KOSHER SALT TO TASTE

Lightly coat a skillet with olive oil. Add the onions, water, and salt to taste. Cover the pan and cook over medium heat, stirring occasionally, until the onions are completely wilted and translucent. Remove the lid and turn the heat up to high. Cook, stirring frequently, until the onions are golden brown and sweet.

Candied Citrus Peel

A USEFUL RECIPE TO HAVE WHEN you want to add a bit of sugared citrus to a dish.

ORANGES OR LEMONS (TO YIELD 1 CUP PEEL)

$1/2$ CUP SUGAR, PLUS SUGAR FOR COATING

$1/4$ CUP WATER

Slice the ends off the fruit so that they can stand sturdily on a cutting board. Using a very sharp paring knife and a downward sawing motion, cut the peel off the fruit in thick strips. Be careful to cut away only the peel, leaving the bitter white pith behind. When you have enough peel to measure 1 cup, cut the strips into a thin julienne.

Place the peel in a small saucepan, cover with cold water, and bring to a simmer. Simmer for about 30 minutes, or until the peel is soft and most of the bitterness is gone. Drain.

Mix the sugar and water together in a small saucepan and bring to a boil, stirring occasionally. When the sugar is completely dissolved add the blanched peel and simmer gently until the peel has absorbed most of the sugar syrup and is translucent. Remove from the pan, and roll in sugar to coat. Lay out on paper towels to dry thoroughly. Store tightly covered.

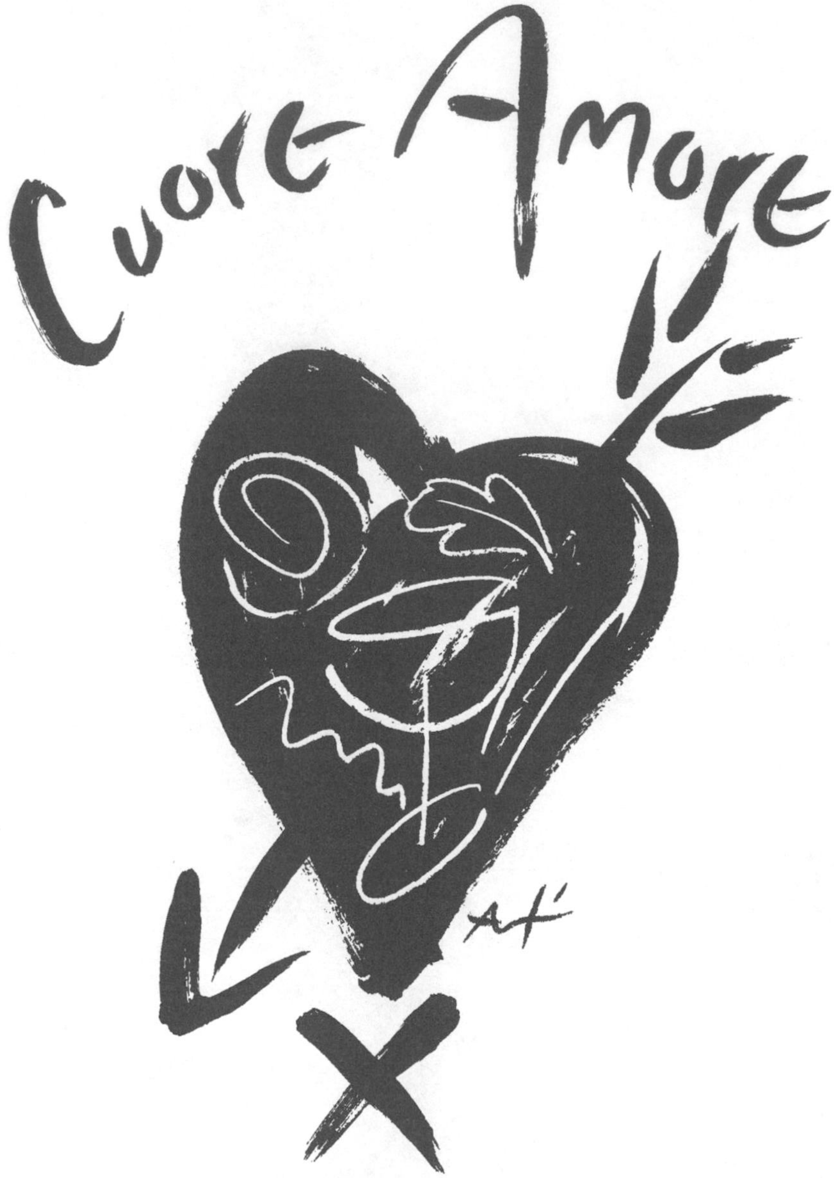
Cuore Amore

bibliography

Alberini, Massimo. *Storia della Cucina Italiana*. Casale Monferrato: Edizioni Piemme, 1992.

Bandera, Maria Teresa. *Super Panini*. Milano: Giovanni De Vecchi, 1987.

Behr, Edward. *The Artful Eater*. New York: The Atlantic Monthly Press, 1992.

Bonacina, Gianni. *Panini & Sandwiches*. Roma: Anthropos, 1983.

Buonassisi, Vincenzo. *Pizza*. Boston: Little Brown, 1984.

Casagrande, Giovanna. *Gola e Preghiera nella Clausura dell'ultimo '500*. Foligno: Edizioni dell'Arquata, 1988.

Codacci, Leo. *Pane, Olio e Vino*. Lucca: Maria Paccini Fazzi, 1991.

La Cucina Italiana: Pizze, Focacce, Torte Salate. Milano: Sperling and Kupfer Editori, 1994.

Della Salda, Anna Gosetti. *Le Ricette Regionali Italiane*. Milano: Casa Editrice "Solares," 1967.

Downie, David. *Saveur: Where Pizza Was Born*. July-August 1995.

Field, Carol. *Focaccia*. San Francisco: Chronicle Books, 1994.

———*The Italian Baker*. New York: HarperCollins, 1985.

Medagliani, Eugenio. *Pastario*. Milano: Alessi, 1985.

Negrone, Josine. *Pizze e Focacce*. Milano: Giovanni di Vecchi, 1986.

Piccinardi, Antonio. *Pizze, Focacce e Tartine*. Milano: Giorgio Mondadori, 1994.

Roggero, Savina. *Cucina Zingara*. Milano: Gruppo Editoriale Fabbri, 1982.

Romer, Elizabeth. *Italian Pizza and Hearth Breads*. New York: Clarkson Potter, 1987.

Sada, Luigi. *La Cucina Pugliese*. Roma: Newton Compton, 1994.

Sloman, Evelyne. *The Pizza Book*. New York: Times Books, 1984.

Thorne, John and Matt. *Simple Cooking*. Food newsletter, Steuben, Maine.

index

S

GRAZIE L.A.
ANGELI